BLACK PEARLS

THE A-Z OF BLACK FOOTBALLERS IN THE ENGLISH GAME

EDITED BY AL HAMILTON WITH RODNEY HINDS

HANSIB

First published in 1999 by Hansib Publications

Hansib Publications Limited
Tower House, 141-149 Fonthill Road,
London N4 3HF, England

A CIP catalogue record of this book is available from the British Library

ISBN 1 870518 71 3

Cover designed by Stefan Brazzo
Production and origination by Graphic Resolutions, Welwyn
Printed and bound in Great Britain by Martins the Printers, Berwick upon Tweed

Foreword

As we approach the 21st Century the role of the Black footballer continues to develop.

Having started my professional football career in England during the late Sixties, when the sight of a Black player was rare to say the least, it is now pleasing to see the constant progress of players from our community.

To see the likes of Sol Campbell and Paul Ince being made captains of the England team should fill us all with a sense of pride and bears testimony to the strides made.

What *Black Pearls* has set out to do is not only highlight the deeds of John Barnes, Andy Cole and Des Walker but also to give prominence to players who played the game throughout all levels of the sport.

The feature on players who played in my era and who have now gone into coaching, management or the media, confirms that Black players - past and present - have a role to play in a sport that continues to grow in its popularity.

Brendon M. Batson
Deputy Chief Executive
Professional Footballers' Association

Al Hamilton

Since the early 1970s, Jamaican-born Al Hamilton has been involved in the world of sport and sporting activities as an author, journalist and promoter. He has written for *West Indian Digest, West Indian World, Caribbean Post* and *The Gleaner*, and was the Sports Editor of the *Caribbean Times*.

Between 1987 and 1994, he organised two soccer tours to Jamaica in a quest to improve the national team. John Barnes took the role of captain and he was assisted by Ian Wright.

In 1993, he brought the Caribbean All Stars to Leyton Orient for a Testimonial game to honour the late Laurie Cunningham. The team featured Jamaican goalkeeper Warren Barrett, who went on to captain Jamaica's national team during the World Cup in France.

In 1978, he founded the Commonwealth Sports Awards, an annual event which celebrates its 21st anniversary in 1999.

Rodney Hinds

Rodney Hinds has commented on sport for the last twenty years. His career in journalism began at the *West Indian World* newspaper where he ascended to Sports Editor during the early Eighties. Since then, he has been a freelance writer for *The Voice* and is currently Chief Sports Writer for *The Journal*.

Football is his first sporting passion but he has a keen interest in athletics, boxing, cricket and netball.

Among the highlights of his two decades in sport, he says the most memorable occasion was when he covered the World Cup match between Argentina and Jamaica during France 98.

Acknowledgements

Grateful thanks to Rodney Hinds, a friend and soul-mate for over twenty years whose contribution to this project is truly noteworthy; Ron Shillingford, Sports Editor of *New Nation*, with whom I have shared some memorable sporting moments; Joan and Clive Fuller, Gloria Rose, Mikey Massive, Alan Ramsey and John Fashanu; Arif Ali and the Hansib team, with special praise to Kash Ali who designed and godfathered the book through all the stages; Seraphina, Cherry-Ann Carew, Tony Laforce and Tony Risveglia; and Fay Nesbeth for being a rock of solid support. *Al Hamilton*

Contents

Introduction

The Black presence among the ranks of Britain's professional footballers is now taken for granted. Indeed, the Black footballer in Europe is a welcome, and unavoidable, fact of life.

The inclusion of players of African heritage in the line-ups of nations as diverse as Sweden, Norway, Holland and, world champions, France bears testimony to the increasingly cosmopolitan nature of, hitherto, rigid categorisation of national identity. It demonstrates, once again, the genius of people of the African diaspora to overcome previously, and seemingly, insurmountable odds to excel and, thereby, court admiration.

Perhaps it should be mentioned early on that many of the players catalogued in this book would, most likely, cringe at their inclusion in a tome with such a perceivably anachronistic title. Managers and coaches invariably select players on the basis of their ability and adjudged compatibility with the other available players in the team, and never by the colour of their skin. Nevertheless, the proliferation of Black players throughout Britain and Europe is a relatively recent phenomenon caused, in no small part, by the changing demands of the modern game.

The performance of soccer at the top level has always required prodigious athletic prowess, as well as technical gifts. Traditionally, European soccer stars have been recruited from the ranks of the underprivileged and working classes - perhaps only they were 'hungry' enough to cultivate their talents by way of the necessary sacrifice and determination to succeed.

Scouts and coaches are compelled to search far and wide to unearth new gems if they wish to keep pace with rivals and competitors. And the antiquated quasi-nepotism of the past has become outmoded in an era where continued success is a prerequisite for keeping employment.

Not so long ago, Everton fans boasted, "Hello, hello, Everton are white, Everton are white," in reference to the Merseyside club's racial homogeneity. The fans soon tired of being the top flight's sole bastion of 'racial purity' as season after season passed and their team failed to win any of the game's much coveted honours. At roughly the same time, a former chairman claimed that he believed that Black players were incapable of performing at the top of their game once the English winter set in. His statement embarrassed and alienated his club's Black players and the subsequent transfers of a handful of Black stars eventually led to the club's relegation.

One need not look back as far as the days of Arthur Wharton or Walter Tull as examples of an era when the Black presence was near negligible; few modern soccer fans aged under 35 would be able to recall how 'colourless' the game was when only Albert Johanneson of Leeds and Clyde

Best of West Ham United were household names in the then First Division. Presently, it is estimated that approximately one third of Britain's professional footballers boast African and Caribbean ancestry.

It is true that the professional footballer is a privileged, perhaps cosseted, individual in Western society. At a time when men and women of a darker hue are treated like pariahs by Western immigration authorities, a football club is able to receive accreditation for youngsters from as far afield as Nigeria, Costa Rica or Guinea-Bissau with hardly the batting of an eyelid.

Nevertheless, not all professional soccer players enjoy the high life. For every household name, such as a Dwight Yorke or Marcel Desailly, there are a host of professionals, no less committed, but plying their trade in relative obscurity. How many fans who do not support Chesterfield Town, Wolverhampton Wanderers, Luton Town, Torquay United or Mansfield Town would be aware of the long service of men such as Roger Willis, Donald Goodman, Mitchell Thomas, Jon Gittens or Tony Ford?

The Black footballer presents one with an opportunity to engage in a microcosmic consideration of the wider Black community with its victories and disappointments placed under the spotlight. And Black Pearls allows us to assess those who have acquitted themselves in glory and those who, outwardly, appear to have acquired few of the game's material benefits but would most likely testify to the satisfaction they have derived for being paid for doing something they truly love.

Pele's beautiful game is, indeed, a funny old game. But we wouldn't have it any other way.

The pioneers who paved the way

Arthur Wharton

Imagine England during the 1880s and a young man, born in Ghana, the son of a Scottish father and an African-Grenadian mother, playing professional football. Arthur Wharton, who arrived in Britain in 1875, joined Preston North End in 1886, two years before the inception of the football league and officially turned 'pro' three years later.

Wharton was a goalkeeper with great agility who took immense pride in his performance. A letter sent to the Sheffield Telegraph and Independent stated: "In a match between Rotherham and Sheffield Wednesday, at Olive Grove, I saw Wharton jump, take hold of the cross bar, catch the ball between his legs, and cause three on-rushing forwards, Billy Ingham, Clinks Mamford and Mickey Bennett, to fall into the net. I have never seen a similar save since and I have been watching football for over fifty years."

Arthur Wharton also served Darlington FC, Rotherham Town, Sheffield United and Stockport County.

Before his colourful career came to a close in 1902, he also won the 100 yards in 10 seconds at the 1886 AAA's Championships at Stamford Bridge.

Arthur Wharton died in December 1930 and he was buried at Ealington near Doncaster.

Walter Tull

Walter Tull was born on 28 April 1888 in Folkestone, Kent. He was one of two sons of a Barbadian father and English mother. But, by the age of nine, and following the death of their parents, Walter and his brother Edward were placed in an orphanage in Bethnal Green, east London. Edward was later adopted by a Scottish family.

Walter (pictured opposite), who remained at the orphanage, shone as a left-back for the orphanage football team. His prowess soon spread resulting in an invitation to join Clapton FC in 1908 aged 20. Before the end of that first year, he had broken into the First XI gaining winners' medals in the FA Amateur Cup, London County Cup and Senior London Cup. His strident contribution and influence to the team was referred to as "the catch of the season".

He starred alongside future Spurs player Charlie Rance, in the FA Amateur Cup Final, 6-0 victory over Eston United. At Ilford in Essex, apprentice forms were signed with north London club Tottenham Hotspur. With only a few reserve games and one first team slot in a friendly, he was invited to join the club tour of South America, visiting Argentina and Uruguay in June 1909.

Tull made his full professional debut

three months later against Sunderland, a game his team lost 3-1 away. He earned £4 per week and was nicknamed "Darkie" by his own fans. A month after, Spurs travelled west to play Bristol City, a section of the home supporters taunted him in what one reporter of the match described as, "language lower than Billingsgate fish market". The article concluded: "Let me tell these Bristol hooligans that Tull is so clean in mind and method, as to be a model for all white men who play football whether they be amateur or professional. In point of ability if not in achievement Tull was the best forward on the field!"

He was off-loaded to Northampton Town (known as the Cobblers) in an exchange deal which saw Richard Britain going to Spurs.

Walter Tull answered the call to serve King and Country in the Great War where he rose to the rank of 2nd Lieutenant - the first and only Black officer in the British army until the Second World War.

He was killed in action during the second battle of the Somme in 1918. He was awarded the British War and Victory Medal. Walter Tull was also recommended for the Military Cross.

Albert Johanneson

In 1965, Albert Johanneson became the first Black player to appear in an FA Cup Final at Wembley. Born on 13 March 1940 in Johannesburg, South Africa, he signed for Leeds United in April 1961. He was joint top scorer during 1964 when Leeds won the Second Division title, and he continued to reek havoc on defences in the First Division. Injuries ended his career at Leeds at the age of 30. He joined York City in July 1970.

By then, the glory days were gone and he returned to South Africa for a spell of coaching which proved unsuccessful.

He came back to England where he lived in Leeds until his death in September 1995.

Steve Mokone

Centre forward, Steve Mokone joined Coventry City in 1956, where he made four appearances and scored once. He moved to Cardiff City in 1959 and played three times scoring once. He also had spells in Holland for Heracles and with Torino in Italy.

At present, a film is being made of Mokone's life which is due out at the end of 1999 called 'Black Meteor'. Away from the camera he is a representative of the South African Tourist Board in the United States and has gained himself a PhD in Community Affairs.

France 98: A gateway to the future

After 64 matches, 171 goals, 22 red cards and 257 yellow cards, hosts, France put their name on the final World Cup of this century after humbling a below par Brazil in the magnificent Stade de France on 12 July 1998.

France's convincing 3-0 win against the holders was the first time in eight meetings that they had managed to overcome the South Americans.

Moroccan midfielder Zinedine Zidane's two soft headers will forever go down in French football history, but it was defender Lilian Thuram's double strike during the semi-final against Croatia, who made it possible.

Thuram (pictured opposite), who plays for Italian Serie A club Parma and has been capped 38 times, could not have chosen a better time to open his international account as the pressurised home team struggled to overcome the tournament's surprise packet.

After going a goal down, Thuram's goals ensured that the dream final - hosts had never met holders before - became a reality.

Thuram, born in the Caribbean, who, without doubt the best right-sided defender during the World Cup, was ably supported in the French defence by Chelsea's Marcel Desailly, who saw red during the final after two bookable offences.

In the engine-room of the French team was Arsenal's Patrick Vieira who had limited opportunities to show his real worth as did Christian Karembeu of Real Madrid.

The French, who got better as the tournament went on, look to have unearthed two promising strikers in the shape of Thierry Henry and David Trezeguet, who at the end of France 98 had just 20 caps between them sharing five goals. But the potential of both players was there for all to see. Goal-scoring has always been a problem for the French but now they appeared to have the solution to their lack of success in front of goal.

Much-hyped Ronaldo and his team mates will want to forget their French affair as soon as possible. Having been in hospital just moments before the biggest match of his life, Ronaldo failed to showcase the talents that were only hinted at in the earlier rounds of the competition.

In truth, Brazil had looked vulnerable throughout France 98 - testimony provided by their shock defeat to Norway in the opening round - and they were there to be taken by any side which had the gall to do so.

Only the much maligned goalkeeper Claudio Taffarel, defender Cafu and midfielders Cesar Sampaio - who scored the first goal of the tournament against Scotland - and Barcelona's Rivaldo, performed with any real conviction.

Once again, Holland's highly gifted

players ended up as unlucky bridesmaids. They played the smoothest football of any of the competing nations, but they were unable to cultivate their impeccable technique into a winning formula.

Star man for the orange men was unquestionably the reformed Edgar Davids of Juventus. Once dubbed a "pit-bull" by a former coach, Davids was the integral member of the classy Dutch midfield. He is sure to add to his sixteen caps and his performances during the World Cup must have gone some way to ease the pain of the European Cup Final defeat he and his club suffered at the hands of Real Madrid in May 1998.

In the Madrid team that beat Juventus was Clarence Seedorf who did not make as much of a stark impression in the Dutch team as Davids, but showed enough skill and energy to mark him down as a potential star for the next tournament to be held in 2002 in Japan and South Korea. Other useful contributors to the Dutch effort, for so long a divided team in the dressing room, was the fleet-footed right-back Michael Reiziger, the unlucky Winston Bogarde - who broke his leg -

veteran Aaron Winter and Premiership marksmen Pierre Van Hooijdonk (Nottingham Forest) and Leeds United's Jimmy Floyd Hasselbaink.

Barcelona's Patrick Kluivert put his recent off-field troubles behind him to announce himself as a striker, who once again, looks to have enough ability to fulfil his potential. His well taken goal against Argentina in the quarter-finals, after a deft header by the mercurial Dennis Bergkamp, signalled that Barcelona's gain came at the expense of Premiership clubs who competed for his signature.

After much expectancy, the five African nations were heading for French airports after their last representatives, Nigeria, were soundly beaten by a rejuvenated Denmark in the round of the last sixteen.

Nigeria, who had one of the stars of the tournament in Austin Jay Jay Okocha, had got off to the perfect start by beating one of the pre-tournament favourites, Spain, 3-2 in Nantes. A rocket of a shot by defender Sunday Oliseh in the 78th minute fuelled false African optimism.

Victory over an ageing but experienced Bulgarian side almost a week later suggested that the vision of an African nation winning the sport's most prestigious trophy held some reality.

Alas, defeat against Paraguay in the last match of the opening round was to prove an indicator of things to come.

Against the Danes, Nigeria decided to play their football AFTER they went two-nil down inside the first quarter of an hour. Against an experienced international side, containing the likes of Peter Schmeichel and the Laudrup brothers, the Nigerians left themselves with a mountain to climb. It proved insurmountable.

Africa's other representatives wished they had got as far as Nigeria. Cameroon, Morocco, South Africa and Tunisia all saw their challenges falter during the first round.

Morocco beat Scotland 3-0 in their final group match but still failed to qualify after Norway unexpectedly beat Brazil to claim the final qualifying berth from Group A.

Cameroon, too, suffered a frustrating exit. They could only draw 1-1 with Chile in their final Group B match and found themselves heading home. And all this after seeing what appeared to be a legitimate goal wiped off the score-sheet by referee Vagner of Hungary.

Much revered striker Benny McCarthy was not able to turn his potential into goals for South Africa. Highlight for the World Cup debutantes was an impressive draw against Denmark in Toulouse. The South Africans showed enough talent and technique to suggest that they could emerge as the next major force from the continent.

Tunisia were destined to be the whipping boys of Group G. They were beaten by England and Colombia but ended their campaign with a creditable draw against the already qualified Romanians.

Overall, it was a disappointing tournament for the African nations. Their showing during France 98 could well see reduced places for their countries in Japan and South Korea at the next World Cup in 2002.

While African footballers play a major role for some of Europe's biggest clubs, there is still some way to go before that talent is turned into an all conquering international unit.

Jamaica's Reggae Boyz were everybody's favourite underdogs during the Finals. After an encouraging performance during their opening Group H defeat against eventual semi-finalists Croatia, the Boyz were then handed the severest of lessons by Argentina.

The South Americans put five goals past the Caribbean island's mixture of home-grown talent and Premiership performers. It was a woeful performance by coach Rene Simoes' team and underlined the step up in class that the Jamaicans had made.

Argentina's Gabriel Batistuta, with a hat-trick, and Ariel Ortega (2), were the executioners on one of the hottest days that Paris had endured for some time.

At least the Boyz were able to end their World Cup debut with a win against Japan! Theodore Whitmore's goals in the 39th and 54th minute restored some pride.

Star performer for Jamaica was young Ricardo Gardner whose efforts resulted in a £1m move to First Division Bolton Wanderers.

After an epic second round encounter against Argentina, England went home as the tournament's unluckiest losers, after yet another penalty shoot-out disappointment.

After the much chronicled sending-off of David Beckham in the 47th minute, England displayed true bulldog spirit to keep Argentina at bay. Central to that effort was Sol Campbell who must have added millions to his transfer value with his stout defending and well-timed tackles. The Tottenham defender even had a goal disallowed as the game in Saint Etienne reached fever pitch.

A game which could have gone either way was eventually decided by the lottery of penalties. Paul Ince was the first Englishman to miss a penalty and then David Batty also caved in to the pressures of scoring from twelve yards and, once again, England were denied in the cruellest possible way.

The sight of Liverpool captain Ince crying at the end of the shoot-out brought home the emotion, tension and pressure of sport played in front of millions of spectators.

France 98 was not a classic by any means, and there were few games that made their way into the competition's all-time hall of fame.

France were worthy winners because as the competition developed they improved with every game.

A bright future under African skies

Although the shared prediction of the great Pele and former England team manager Walter Winterbottom, concerning an African nation lifting the World Cup before the end of the 20th Century has not been achieved in physical terms, the rise of currency of the African footballer is one of the most remarkable stories in modern sport.

Liberian goal ace George Weah has emerged as African football's most instantly recognisable face over the past few years. However, his success as an African in Europe is by no means isolated and his eminence has provided the template for the proliferation of African talent that is set to continue.

While we may well have seen the best of Weah, the same cannot be said of South Africa's goal-scoring sensation Benedict McCarthy. McCarthy first rose to prominence in the 1997 African Under-21 Championships in Morocco. He was top scorer in that tournament and has since gone on to prove that initial claim to fame was no fluke. The 21-year old, who earns his living with Ajax of Amsterdam, became his national side's top scorer - with seven goals - as they reached the final of the African Nations Cup. They eventually lost 2-0 to Egypt in the final.

McCarthy signalled his intent very early in the highly competitive African competition. In South Africa's opening game against Namibia, this product of Hanover Park, Cape Town, became the first South African international to score a hat-trick in full-blooded competition.

McCarthy's move to Ajax put him in the millionaire bracket; his international coach, Jomo Sono, fully understands why his protégé is now potentially worth millions. "Benni has everything. He makes things happen. He's class."

Nigeria's luckless quarter-final defeat against Italy during USA 94, served notice that here was a team that sooner, rather than later, would capture a major prize. They achieved exactly that when they beat Brazil and Argentina to win the Olympic gold at the 1996 Atlanta Games.

Although the team failed to sustain their early promise at France 98, Nigerian footballers are being called to make contributions to the realisation of ambitions harboured by coaches from all four corners of the globe.

The man at the hub of the Nigerian defence is Uche Okechukwu who plays for top Turkish side Fenerbache. Also enjoying his own Turkish delight is striker Daniel Amokachi of Besiktas, who did as much as anyone to help get Everton to the Cup Final in 1995 during his brief stay with the Premiership club. Amokachi's international strike partners include Jonathan Akpoborie who plays for Stuttgart in Germany and Emmanuel Ammunike who is the darling of Barcelona's fans.

Inter Milan can call upon the services of Taribo West, while Arsenal eventually captured the signature of Nwankwo Kanu (pictured) in January 1998.

Kanu is returning to something like his best form following surgery to arrest a heart defect. And it was outstanding form all season that led to AS Monaco's Victor Ikpeba receiving the coveted African Footballer of the Year Award of 1998. The wonder goal Ikpeba scored against Bulgaria at France 98 enhanced his international profile, following the gritty displays for Monaco that effectively terminated Manchester United's Champions League ambitions for yet another year in March 1998.

In Spain goalkeeper Peter Rufai is the last line of defence for La Coruna. Real Betis reached the quarter-finals of the 1998 European Cup-Winners Cup with midfield ace Finidi George among their number.

Defender Austin Eguavoen has planted the Nigerian flag in the Soviet Republic, where he plies his trade with Torpedo Moscow.

South Africa based its recent first World Cup challenge on the experience of striker Phil Masinga, now with Bari of Italy's Serie A, after a spell with Leeds United. Still with Leeds, however, is South Africa's captain, Lucas Radebe, who recently signed a new long-term contract.

Leeds fans continue to speak in reverential tones about Ghanaian Tony Yeboah who captured their collective imagination after signing for the Yorkshire club in January 1995. He illuminated stadiums with his predatory skills in front of goal. Yeboah made just 59 appearances for United but scored 32 times. He was to win BBC TV's 1996 Goal of the Season Award after a memorable left foot thunderbolt against Liverpool.

Fellow Ghanaian Abedi Pele brought the curtain down on his illustrious career after his country's dismal showing in the 1998 African Nations Cup. Pele, helped his country win the competition in 1982, and he subsequently won the African Player of the Year award three times.

In the Premiership and Nationwide League, Africans continue to make their mark. Injury has ensured that we have not yet seen the best of Chelsea's Celestine Babayaro and Efan Ekoku of Wimbledon, but both are young enough to hold hopes of glory days ahead.

Zimbabwean Peter Ndlovu's scintillating form has been a major contributing factor in First Division Birmingham City's blood and guts bid to achieve Premiership status in England.

Top French side, Paris St Germain have set up a school of excellence, known as Planete Champion, in Burkina Faso, venue for the most recent African Nations Cup. The school intends to nurture the outstanding youngsters coming off Africa's relentless football production line.

Twenty-five students are selected from throughout the continent. They are then provided with academic schooling in the morning and training sessions in the afternoon.

Strong footholds continue to be made by African footballers, both domestically and internationally, and the tide of African nations vying for supremacy cannot be resisted. With South Africa looking likely to stage the 2006 World Cup, there is a bright future under African skies.

The Reggae Boyz and the English connection

Jamaica's national football team, affectionately known as the Reggae Boyz, have brought some welcome respite to the followers of sport in the Caribbean region. While the West Indies cricket team falters at home and abroad, the Reggae Boyz have stood out like beacons.

France 98 danced to the beat of a new drum as Jamaica's compelling reggae rhythms signalled that a Caribbean nation had reached the latter stages of the greatest show on earth for the first time.

The Parc des Princes in Paris witnessed hundreds of Jamaican supporters looking forward to an encounter against Argentina, previous winners of the World Cup.

It did not matter that some ninety minutes later, the Reggae Boyz would be at the wrong end of a 5-0 thrashing, the message was loud and clear: football is now big news in Jamaica, in particular, and the rest of the Caribbean islands, in general.

Intriguingly, it is English-based players - those performing in the Premiership and Football League - that are at the hub of Jamaica's transition to international football.

There might have been less to cheer had it not been for the likes of Wimbledon's Robbie Earle and Marcus Gayle, Leicester City's Frank Sinclair, the goals of Derby County's Deon Burton, the grit and determination of Portsmouth's Fitzroy Simpson and Coventry City's Paul Hall.

Robbie Earle, captain of his south-east London club, led from the front. As for Deon Burton (left), his goals almost single-handedly took Jamaica to the World Cup.

Dubbed 'One Love' after the Bob Marley song, Burton scored on his debut against Canada and also against Costa Rica, goals that saw his 'adopted' country eke out 1-0 victories. As if that were not enough, Burton scored in late 1997 against the United States in a 1-1 draw and put the icing on the cake with another goal in the last and vital qualifier against El Salvador. That 2-2 draw saw the Reggae Boyz book their passage to France.

Although the contribution of the English connection has been immense, there is a reciprocal acknowledgement of the capabilities of their team-mates, as befits a sport that relies on individualism but has, at its foundations, the team-work ethic.

One player who has joined the English ranks is the highly talented Ricardo

Gardner, who impressed tremendously while in football's biggest shop window in France. His services have been snapped up by Bolton Wanderers who, at the start of 1999, look likely to regain their Premiership status after a sojourn in the Nationwide First Division.

Transferred from the Harbour View Club in Jamaica, Gardner has not been able to command a first team place in the northern club, but his time will surely come.

While Gardner has been able to get a foot-hold in the English game some of his international team-mates have not yet made the grade. Ian Goodison and Theodore Whitmore, whose brace of goals against Japan saw the Caribbean outfit end their World Cup dream with a victory, have both had trials in England that have not been cemented.

As yet, no Premiership club has enlisted the services of a home-grown Reggae Boy.

Jamaican football needs to push on after the glory of France 98, never mind the final results. For that continued development to progress, Jamaican-born players will need to be sought and amalgamated with their English connections. It is that potent mix of raw talent and English professionalism that made them everyone's favourite underdog in France.

However, once that novelty wears off the serious business of making strides in the international game becomes paramount, otherwise the decline of the region's cricketers could be mirrored if the administrators and players do not learn from the lessons of the last World Cup.

Management: The final frontier

Ruud Gullit's shock, and undignified, departure from Chelsea in February 1998 confirmed, in no uncertain terms, the fickle nature of football management. Only months earlier, Gullit (pictured right) had helped the club win the FA Cup, its first major honour in over two decades. The first Black Premiership manager had also steered The Blues to a European Cup-Winners Cup quarter-final and a League Cup semi-final (which they subsequently won under new player manager GianLuca Vialli) and a genuine, challenging position in the Carling Premiership when the club decided to dispense with Gullit's services.

Chris Kamara suffered the ignominy of the sack from his post at Bradford City - this, just months after staving off the very genuine threat of the club playing in the Second Division. No more than two weeks later Stoke City boss Chic Bates was moved sideways (to the position of first-team coach) with Kamara taking his place. In April 1998, Kamara resigned from Stoke City as they headed woefully towards the Second Division of the Nationwide League.

The advancement of Black players over the last twenty years has led to some of yesterday's pioneers taking the 'natural' step of coaching or management. A glance at the staff listings across the four divisions conjures up the names of retired stars who have swapped their playing kits for tracksuits.

Apart from Gullit's efforts with Chelsea, and now with Newcastle United, in the Premiership, Chris Hughton - capped 53 times by the Republic of Ireland and an FA Cup winner at Tottenham Hotspur - flies the flag for Black coaches as the assistant to Tottenham manager George Graham in north London. Also in the top flight with Sheffield Wednesday is Ricky Hill (left), who had previously won three England caps and a League Cup winners medal with Luton Town.

Middlesbrough manager Bryan Robson is assisted by

Viv Anderson (above, left) who, in 1978, became the first Black footballer to play for England. In a decade with Brian Clough's Nottingham Forest, Anderson won it all - a Division One Championship medal, two European Cups and two League Cups. His input has guided Boro to three successive Wembley Cup Finals over the last two seasons along with Premiership respectability.

Former West Bromwich Albion favourite, Cyrille Regis (above, centre) has returned to his old club as coach to support manager Denis Smith's bid to get them back into the big time.

Former Watford striker, Luther Blissett (above, right) is another Black coach doing his bit at a club he once represented. Blissett, who also tasted the good life briefly with Italian giants AC Milan, is in tandem with former England manager Graham Taylor, as the two attempt to return Watford to the big time. Blissett made his international debut for England in 1983 coming on as a sub against West Germany. He went on to wear the England shirt on another 13 occasions.

Should John Barnes (currently on loan to Charlton Athletic from Newcastle United) decide against a TV pundit's role, one could see him fitting comfortably into the coaching side of the game. So, too, Des Walker of Sheffield Wednesday, Chris Fairclough of Notts County and Clive Wilson of Tottenham.

These players are all in the twilight of their careers, but each one possesses the vast experience required and, above all, the respect of their peers.

The next step would be the appointment of the first, home-grown Black manager. Watch this space!

Beyond the field of dreams

Many former players who have decided that the dagger-in-the-back existence of a coach or manager is not for them, have carved out careers that allow them contact with the game.

Brendon Batson, the Deputy Chief Executive of the Professional Footballers Association, was ironically sent off early in his career with Cambridge United when he struck out at an opponent who had continually called him a "black bastard" during a match with Stockport County. He is now the man who uses his experience and cultivated knowledge to help players with their on and off field problems.

Batson, who came to Britain aged nine, gained the expertise required to carry out his present duties as a hard-tackling full back not only at Cambridge, but also with Arsenal, West Bromwich Albion and as an England B international.

Another defender, albeit slightly more uncompromising, was Bob Hazell. Hazell, formerly with Wolverhampton Wanderers and Queens Park Rangers, was revered at the clubs he played for due to his positive energy and will to win. Now he is working with youngsters keen on football at Aston Villa Football Club.

Paul Elliott and Garth Crooks are now both regular faces on TV screens. Elliott, whose promising career with Chelsea was prematurely cut short by injury, now employs his fluency in Italian to talk a good game as a resident expert on Channel 4's 'Football Gazetta' series. And Crooks, a striker with Stoke City and Tottenham Hotspur, is forging a career as a TV journalist in sport and politics where he is just as comfortable giving analyses on 'Match of the Day' and 'Football Focus' as he is on 'Despatch Box'.

Throughout his career, Garth Crooks was the most prominent sporting representative for the Sickle Cell Anaemia Research organisation.

Danny Thomas is now one of the leading authorities on sports injury/medicine in the Midlands. Thomas wore the colours of Coventry City and Tottenham Hotspur with distinction and was regarded by many as one of the best right backs to represent England over the past twenty years, before a crippling knee injury forced him into early retirement.

Former Southampton player George Lawrence has also gone into sports medicine, running his own practice in Birmingham.

John Fashanu, a former presenter on 'Gladiators', has left behind the stigma of match-rigging allegations to become Nigeria's roving Ambassador for Sport, with a portfolio to promote the country's abundance of sporting talent and also generate funds for the African nation's sporting coffers. He is also a UNICEF Ambassador.

Beware the man in black

Jamaican-born Uriah Rennie became the Carling Premiership's first Black referee during the 1997/98 season. After topping the Nationwide League merit table for referees the season before, he was promoted to the Premiership for his competent performances.

His introduction to the Premiership could not have been more fraught! He was the man in charge for the Derby County against Wimbledon match in August 1997. Mid-way through the second half the floodlights failed, compelling him to abandon the match, which ironically was the first staged at Derby's new state-of-the-art Pride Park stadium.

Rennie, who spends his days as a 'civilian' as the operations manager of the Hillsborough Sports Centre in Sheffield, demands respect with his powerful frame, strong features and calm, but commanding, vocal presence.

Anyone who has seen Rennie in action during his first couple of Premiership seasons comes away with the impression that he is not a man to be meddled with. A reason for that almost judicial-like respect, may stem from the fact that Rennie is a practising Justice of the Peace. And as if that was not enough to make would-be transgressors think twice, Rennie is also a keen kick-boxer.

Presently renowned, primarily, for being the first and only Black top-flight officiator, Rennie is fast forging a reputation as one of the most competent and physically capable referees in the English game. International duties cannot be far behind.

Nathaniel Abbey

LUTON TOWN

Goalkeeper

Nationality: English
Place of Birth: London
Date of Birth: 11 July 1978
Height: 6'1"

Samassi Abou

WEST HAM UNITED

Forward

Nationality: French
Place of Birth: Ivory Coast
Date of Birth: 4 April 1973
Height: 5'8"
Club History: Cannes
Ipswich Town
Bradford City
Honours/Caps: Caps for Ivory Coast

The West Ham manager, Harry Rednapp, first spotted Samassi Abou in 1995 playing for the Ivory Coast during the Toulon Under-21 tournament and signed him from French club Cannes for £300,000.

The Hammers' boss is not known for his success with international signings, but he saw something in the youngster that caught his eye, and backed his hunch with his cheque book... only to be accosted by a chorus of doubters!

Following a series of unconvincing performances as substitute, Abou settled in and began silencing his critics as well as those who questioned Redknapp's judgement.

Samassi broke his duck with his first goal for the Hammers against Arsenal during the fourth round of the Coca Cola Cup in 1997. Although West Ham suffered a 2-1 defeat, Abou's dynamic display gave the fans a taste of things to come.

Bamberdele Adebola

BIRMINGHAM CITY

Forward

Nationality: English
Place of Birth: Liverpool
Date of Birth: 23 June 1975
Height: 6'3"
Club History: Crewe Alexandra

Adeola Akinbiyi

BRISTOL CITY

Forward

Nationality: English
Place of Birth: London
Date of Birth: 10 October 1974
Height: 6'1"
Club History: Norwich City
Hereford United
Brighton & Hove Albion
Gillingham

Colin Alcide

LINCOLN CITY

Midfielder

Nationality: English
Place of Birth: Huddersfield
Date of Birth: 14 April 1972
Height: 6'2"
Club History: Emley

Chris Allen

NOTTINGHAM FOREST

Forward

Nationality: English
Place of Birth: Oxford
Date of Birth: 18 November 1972
Height: 5'11"
Club History: Oxford United
Honours/Caps: England Under 21

Samassi Abou

Bamberdele Adebola

Wayne Allison

HUDDERSFIELD TOWN

Forward

Nationality: English
Place of Birth: Huddersfield
Date of Birth: 16 October 1968
Height: 6'1"
Club History: Halifax Town
Watford
Bristol City
Swindon Town

Kwame Ampadu

SWANSEA CITY

Forward

Nationality: English
Place of Birth: Bradford
Date of Birth: 20 December 1970
Height: 5'10"
Club History: Arsenal
Plymouth Argyle
West Bromwich Albion

Ijah Anderson

BRENTFORD

Defender

Nationality: English
Place of Birth: London
Date of Birth: 30 December 1975
Height: 5'8"
Club History: Tottenham Hotspur
Southend United

Wayne Andrews

WATFORD

Forward

Nationality: English
Place of Birth: London
Date of Birth: 25 January 1977
Height: 5'10"

Nicolas Anelka

ARSENAL

Forward

Nationality: French
Place of Birth: Versailles
Date of Birth: 24 March 1979
Height: 6'0"
Club History: Paris St Germain
Honours/Caps: Premiership 1998 with Arsenal
FA Cup 1998 with Arsenal
Caps for France at all levels

Purchased by Arsenal in March 1997, Nicolas Anelka has gone a long way to fill the space left in the heart of the Gunners by the departure of the legendary Ian Wright.

Formerly with Paris St. Germain, Anelka is known for his devastating pace. His all-round skill played an instrumental role in Arsenal's triumphant 1998 Premiership and FA Cup Double campaign. In the view of many experts Anelka was very unlucky to miss out on a place with France during the 1998 World Cup.

Arsenal coach, Arsene Wenger has few qualms concerning his talented young countryman: "Nicolas will be the striker of the future for Arsenal. He has all the assets that a striker needs. He combines physical power with his height and speed. He is also flexible, and to have all those qualities in one player is rare."

Paul Anthrobus

CREWE ALEXANDRA

Forward

Nationality: English
Place of Birth: London
Date of Birth: 10 November 1968
Height: 6'2"
Club History: Millwall
Southend United
Wimbledon
Peterborough United
Chester City
Shrewsbury Town

Nicolas Anelka

Chris Armstrong

TOTTENHAM HOTSPUR

Forward

Nationality: English
Place of Birth: Newcastle
Date of Birth: 19 June 1971
Height: 6'0"
Club History: Wrexham
Millwall
Crystal Palace
Honours/Caps: First Division Championship 1994 with Crystal Palace
One Cap for England B

When Chris Armstrong signed for Tottenham in June 1995 for a cool £4.5m, the immediate pressure on the formerly prolific Crystal Palace striker was two-fold. Firstly, he was bought as a replacement for fans' favourite, Jurgen Klinsmann, and secondly, he had to justify the club's then record fee with goals. He started well enough but injuries hampered him during the 1997/98 season. He came back to something like his best form during the 1998/99 season.

Pegguy Arphexad

LEICESTER CITY

Goalkeeper

Nationality: French
Place of Birth: Guadeloupe
Date of Birth: 18 May 1973
Height: 6'2"
Club History: R C Lens
Honours/Caps: France Under 21s

Carl Asaba

READING

Forward

Nationality: English
Place of Birth: London
Date of Birth: 28 January 1973
Height: 6'2"
Club History: Brentford
Colchester United

Kevin Austin

LINCOLN CITY

Defender

Nationality: English
Place of Birth: London
Date of Birth: 12 February 1973
Height: 6'0"
Club History: Leyton Orient

Celestine Babayaro

CHELSEA

Defender

Nationality: Nigerian
Place of Birth: Nigeria
Date of Birth: 29 August 1978
Height: 5'7"
Club History: Anderlecht
Honours/Caps: Caps for Nigeria
Belgian League Championship 1995 with Anderlecht
Olympic Gold 1996
League Cup 1998
European Cup Winners Cup 1998 for Chelsea

How many footballers have achieved as many honours as this fleet-footed, left-back from Nigeria at the tender age of twenty? While many young professionals begin by establishing reputations at their clubs, Celestine Babayaro - who celebrates each of his goals with a somersault - already has a track record that would overshadow many veteran players.

He was a member of the Nigerian Under-17 team which won the gold medal at the 1993 World Championships in Japan and then he struck gold again with the Nigerian team that beat all-conquering Argentina in the Final of the 1996 Atlanta Olympics. It was Babayaro's flying header that sealed victory against the South American giants.

Those heady days of glory followed his period of apprenticeship with Nigerian clubs Rancher Bees and Plateau United. From there he travelled to Belgium and joined the

Chris Armstrong fends off West Ham's Rio Ferdinand

Celestine Babayaro

internationally renowned Anderlecht, much to the disappointment of his parents who wanted him to carve out a professional career in law or medicine.
However, Babayaro was convinced which route he intended to take, and has more than proved himself on the field of play with continuing success.
While at Anderlecht he won a Championship medal as well as the Young Player of the Year Award in 1995. And in 1996 he won the Ebony Boot Award, an acknowledgement given to the best African player in the Belgian league.
Now at Chelsea, after a £2.25m move in 1997, he is under the stewardship of Luca Vialli, one of his childhood heroes. The west London club, with the all-star international line-up, are set to make a serious challenge for the Premiership title, and with Celestine Babayaro on side, more acrobatics are in store.

Phil Babb

LIVERPOOL

Defender

Nationality: Irish
Place of Birth: London
Date of Birth: 30 November 1970
Height: 6'0"
Club History: Millwall
Bradford City
Coventry City
Honours/Caps: League Cup 1995 with Liverpool
Caps for Republic of Ireland

Phil Babb started his career with Millwall and then went on to play for Bradford and Coventry City before signing for Liverpool in 1994 for £3.6m.
Babb is a thoughtful and solid defender and, as an established international with the Republic of Ireland, he has always been regarded as a valuable player. But at Liverpool he is just one of a host of defenders in an all-star squad and he has found it increasingly difficult to maintain a regular place in the first team.

Dennis Bailey

LINCOLN CITY

Forward

Nationality: English
Place of Birth: London
Date of Birth: 13 November 1965
Height: 5'1"
Club History: Fulham
Crystal Palace
Bristol Rovers
Birmingham City
Queens Park Rangers
Charlton Athletic
Brentford
Gillingham
Watford

Ibrahima Bakayoko

EVERTON

Forward

Nationality: Cote D'Ivoire
Place of Birth: Sequela, Ivory Coast
Date of Birth: 31 December 1976
Height: 6'3"
Club History: Montpellier

Everton's search for a top quality striker to partner since departed Duncan Ferguson, ended in October 1998 when they bought Ibrahima Bakayoko for £4.5m from French club Montpellier.
He opened his Everton account with an extra-time goal away to Middlesbrough in the Worthington Cup.

Simon Baldry

HUDDERSFIELD TOWN

Forward

Nationality: English
Place of Birth: Huddersfield
Date of Birth: 12 February 1976
Height: 5'11"

Phil Babb

Ademola Bankole

QUEENS PARK RANGERS

Goalkeeper

Nationality: Nigerian/English
Place of Birth: Nigeria
Date of Birth: 9 September 1969
Height: 6'3"
Club History: Doncaster Rovers
Leyton Orient
Crewe Alexandra

Dominic Barclay

BRISTOL CITY

Midfielder

Nationality: English
Place of Birth: Bristol
Date of Birth: 5 September 1976
Height: 5'10"

John Barnes

CHARLTON ATHLETIC

Midfielder

Nationality: English
Place of Birth: Jamaica
Date of Birth: 7 November 1963
Height: 5'11"
Club History: Watford
Liverpool
Newcastle United
Honours/Caps: First Division Championship 1988 and 1990 with Liverpool
FA Cup 1989 with Liverpool
League Cup 1995 with Liverpool
79 Caps for England

John Barnes is in the twilight of what has been a magnificent career. He is still the most successful and well-known England-based Black player in international football.

Barnes was acquired from non-league Sudbury Court by Watford and it was the team's then manager, former England boss Graham Taylor, who was to play a crucial role in nurturing the young star.

Aided by the legendary Luther Blissett, who acted as 'big brother' to the fledgling newcomer, Barnes soon became the player to watch. With 292 League and Cup appearances and 84 goals under his belt, Barnes had aided his team's progress from the Fourth to the First Division.

But the Hertfordshire club was unable to hold on to their pearl and he was bought by Liverpool, where it was the turn of Kenny Dalglish to continue the development of this mercurial player.

It was during his many years at Liverpool that John Barnes became a household name and a byword for intelligent and cultivated soccer artistry. In 407 games, he scored 108 times; he was awarded Player of the Year by the Professional Footballers Association in 1988; and he won the Football Writers Player of the Year award in 1988 and 1990.

On the international stage, Barnes gained seventy nine caps for England, the highlight being, perhaps, his solo goal against Brazil in 1984 at the Maracana Stadium.

John Barnes has been an inspiration to many young footballers, and his contribution to the English game has been extraordinary.

Jamie Barnwell-Edinboro

CAMBRIDGE UNITED

Forward

Nationality: English
Place of Birth: Hull
Date of Birth: 26 December 1975
Height: 5'1"
Club History: Coventry City
Swansea
Wigan Athletic

John Barnes

Earl Barrett

Earl Barrett

SHEFFIELD WEDNESDAY

Defender

Nationality:	English
Place of Birth:	Rochdale
Date of Birth:	28 April 1967
Height:	5'10"
Club History:	Manchester City Chester City Oldham Athletic Aston Villa Sheffield United Everton
Honours/Caps:	League Cup 1994 with Aston Villa Caps for England

Earl Barrett's finest hour-and-a-half came as a member of the Aston Villa side which, with a 3-1 victory in the Coca-Cola Cup final, halted Manchester United's attempt at a unique domestic treble. This landmark in his career is closely followed by three Caps for England.

It was while at Oldham Athletic that Barrett acquired a taste for giant-killing - usually in Cup competitions. The team, whose valiant players never bothered to read the script, became the underdog favourites of all neutrals.

Barrett's first club - Manchester City - was unable to cultivate his potential and he was loaned to nearby Chester City in March 1986. In November the following year City sold him to Oldham for a less than respectable sum of £35,000.

However, City's loss was Oldham's gain and, under the astute Joe Royle, Barrett became an essential member of the team.

A little over four years later, he was sold to Aston Villa for £1.7m, who later sold him to Everton in January 1995 for the same amount.

Everton had a difficult time holding on to their Premiership status and Barrett's position was also under threat. Days into 1998 he joined First Division Sheffield United in a loan deal, but less than two months later he was involved in a free transfer to Sheffield Wednesday at the hands of then Owls boss, Ron Atkinson.

Chris Bart-Williams

NOTTINGHAM FOREST

Midfielder

Nationality:	English
Place of Birth:	Sierra Leone
Date of Birth:	16 June 1974
Height:	5'11"
Club History:	Leyton Orient Sheffield Wednesday
Honours/Caps:	First Division Championship 1998 with Nottingham Forest Cap for England B

Former England B player, Chris Bart-Williams was instrumental in helping Nottingham Forest out of the First Division and into the top-flight for the 1998/99 season.

His career started at Leyton Orient who sold him to Sheffield Wednesday in 1991 for £275,000.

After 153 appearances for the steel city club, pastures new beckoned in the shape of Nottingham Forest, who splashed out £2.5m for the perceptive midfielder.

Darren Beckford

WALSALL

Forward

Nationality:	English
Place of Birth:	Manchester
Date of Birth:	12 May 1967
Height:	6'1"
Club History:	Manchester City Bury Port Vale Norwich City Oldham Athletic Preston North End

Anthony Bedeau

TORQUAY UNITED

Forward

Nationality:	English
Place of Birth:	London
Date of Birth:	24 March 1979
Height:	5'10"

Chris Bart-Williams

Trevor Benjamin

CAMBRIDGE UNITED

Midfielder

Nationality: English
Place of Birth: Kettering
Date of Birth: 8 February 1979
Height: 6'2"

Frank Bennett

BRISTOL ROVERS

Forward

Nationality: English
Place of Birth: Birmingham
Date of Birth: 3 January 1969
Height: 5'7"
Club History: Southampton
Shrewsbury Town

Gary Bennett

SCARBOROUGH

Defender

Nationality: English
Place of Birth: Manchester
Date of Birth: 4 December 1961
Height: 6'1"
Club History: Manchester City
Cardiff City
Sunderland
Carlisle United

Christopher Billy

PLYMOUTH ARGYLE

Forward

Nationality: English
Place of Birth: Huddersfield
Date of Birth: 2 January 1973
Height: 5'11"
Club History: Huddersfield Town

Mark Blake

WALSALL

Defender

Nationality: English
Place of Birth: Nottingham
Date of Birth: 16 December 1970
Height: 5'11"
Club History: Aston Villa
Wolverhampton Wanderers
Portsmouth
Leicester City

Nathan Blake

BLACKBURN ROVERS

Forward

Nationality: Welsh
Place of Birth: Cardiff
Date of Birth: 27 January 1972
Height: 5'11"
Club History: Cardiff City
Sheffield United
Bolton Wanderers
Honours/Caps: First Division 1997 with Bolton Wanderers
Caps for Wales

One of the main reasons why Bolton Wanderers enjoyed Premiership status in the 1997/98 season was the goal-scoring exploits of Nathan Blake. He scored 19 First Division goals for the Lancashire club during their championship-winning season and subsequent ascent to the top-flight.
Blake first honed his goal-scoring aptitude at his hometown club, Cardiff City. In 131 games the Welsh international scored 35 times.
He then moved to Sheffield United where he would endear himself to a new tribe of local fans by scoring 34 goals in just 69 appearances for the steel city club.
Bolton were next in line to invest in Blake's sharp-shooting skills, and he did not betray their faith in him. However, even with his exceptional ability, the club was unable to secure a second season in the Premiership and they were relegated back to the First Division in May 1998.

Nathan Blake while at Bolton Wanderers

It was an international duty stint for Wales that led to Nathan Blake hitting the headlines once again, although not for his goal-scoring.
Blake alleged that during training, Wales manager, Bobby Gould, made racist remarks towards him. Gould claimed his comments were "acceptable banter", widely used in footballing circles. Blake, of course, did not agree and threatened never to play for Wales again.
"Racism is a thing of the past," he said. "We're in international football. I'm an established striker and I should not have to listen to it from my own people, especially a manager I play for."
After a swift apology from Gould and an enquiry by the Welsh Football Association, the matter appeared to dissolve with few apparent lasting consequences. Early into the 1998/99 season, Blake was signed for £4.25m by Blackburn Rovers.

Noel Blake

EXETER CITY

Defender

Nationality: Jamaican
Place of Birth: Jamaica
Date of Birth: 12 January 1962
Height: 6'0"
Club History: Aston Villa
Shrewsbury Town
Birmingham City
Portsmouth
Leeds United
Stoke City
Bradford City
Dundee United

Luis Boa Morte

ARSENAL

Forward

Nationality: Portuguese
Place of Birth: Lisbon
Date of Birth: 4 August 1977
Height: 5'10"
Club History: Sporting Lisbon
Lourihanense

George Boateng

COVENTRY CITY

Midfielder

Nationality: Dutch
Place of Birth: Ghana
Date of Birth: 5 September 1975
Height: 5'9"
Club History: Feyenoord
Honours/Caps: Caps for Holland Under 21s

Mommanais Bokoto

BRISTOL CITY

Forward

Nationality: French
Place of Birth: France
Date of Birth: 20 October 1974
Height: 5'11"
Club History: Maria Aalter
Manchester United

Thierry Bonalair

NOTTINGHAM FOREST

Defender

Nationality: French
Place of Birth: Paris
Date of Birth: 14 June 1966
Height: 5'9"
Club History: Nantes
Auxerre
Lille
Neuchatel Xamax

Robert Bowry

MILLWALL

Midfielder

Nationality: English
Place of Birth: London
Date of Birth: 19 May 1971
Height: 5'9"
Club History: Queens Park Rangers
Crystal Palace
Honours/Caps: First Division Champions 1994
with Crystal Palace

Leon Braithwaite

EXETER CITY

Forward

Nationality:	English
Place of Birth:	London
Date of Birth:	17 December 1972
Height:	5'11"

Rufus Brevett

FULHAM

Defender

Nationality:	English
Place of Birth:	Derby
Date of Birth:	24 September 1969
Height:	5'8"
Club History:	Doncaster Rovers Queens Park Rangers

Mark Bright

CHARLTON ATHLETIC

Forward

Nationality:	English
Place of Birth:	Stoke
Date of Birth:	6 June 1962
Height:	6'1"
Club History:	Port Vale Leicester City Crystal Palace Sheffield Wednesday Sion Millwall

When Crystal Palace bought Mark Bright from Leicester City in November 1986, they could not have realised how well their investment would turn out. Bright was to forge a partnership with the relatively unknown striker Ian Wright, and soon the sparks began to fly. The pair created an irresistible penalty-box combination which became unstoppable as Palace began to mix it up with the big boys.

In total, Bright scored 112 goals for the Eagles and saw his team through to an FA Cup final in 1990. Even though they were defeated by Manchester United following a replay, the contest was one of the club's greatest achievements.

Bright is one the most experienced players in the Premiership but, unlike Ian Wright, he has not made major headlines since leaving Crystal Palace.

Although he is in the twilight of his career at Charlton, veteran soccer fans will never forget his role in one of English football's most dynamic and effective strike partnerships.

Bright has already forged inroads for his post-football career as a TV pundit with Channel 4's, The Big Breakfast.

Anthony Briscoe

SHREWSBURY TOWN

Forward

Nationality:	English
Place of Birth:	Birmingham
Date of Birth:	16 August 1978
Height:	5'10"

Jason Brisset

AFC BOURNEMOUTH

Forward

Nationality:	English
Place of Birth:	London
Date of Birth:	7 September 1974
Height:	5'10"
Club History:	Arsenal Peterborough United

George Boateng

Marlon Broomes

BLACKBURN ROVERS

Defender

Nationality:	English
Place of Birth:	Birmingham
Date of Birth:	28 November 1977
Height:	6'0"
Club History:	Swindon Town
Honours/Caps:	England Under 21

Since the arrival of new Blackburn Rovers manager Brian Kidd midway through the 1998/99 season, Marlon Broomes has been given the chance to show the ability that has seen him win honours at England Under-21, youth and school levels. He is a powerfully-built defender who contributed fully to the upturn in his team's fortunes in January and February 1999. The one blip on his record during the Kidd renaissance was his sending off in a high-octane match against Chelsea.
Nevertheless, Broomes has left his mark with the distinct possibility that further international honours are not too far away.

Wes Brown

MANCHESTER UNITED

Defender

Nationality:	British
Place of Birth:	Manchester
Date of Birth:	16 March 1979
Height:	6'1"

Wes Brown is the latest gem unearthed from Manchester United's youth academy. The young Brown has so impressed Alex Ferguson that the manager personally conducted negotiations to secure his signature on a five-year contract. The tall 20-year-old has given several excellent performances at right back and impressed all with his pace, assurance and maturity. However, most pundits predicting a long international career, feel his best position will be at centre-half. With the quality of players at Old Trafford it is hard to see how Wes Brown will not progress along the same line as Beckham, Scholes and Butt, and to the England team after gaining a sack full of medals with the Red Devils.

Michael Brown

SHREWSBURY TOWN

Forward

Nationality:	English
Place of Birth:	Birmingham
Date of Birth:	8 February 1968
Height:	5'9"
Club History:	Bolton Wanderers
	Preston North End
	Rochdale

Marvin Bryan

BLACKPOOL

Forward

Nationality:	English
Place of Birth:	London
Date of Birth:	2 August 1975
Height:	6'0"
Club History:	Queens Park Rangers
	Doncaster Rovers

Deon Burton

Danny Cadamarteri

Deon Burton

DERBY COUNTY

Forward

Nationality:	English
Place of Birth:	Reading
Date of Birth:	25 October 1976
Height:	5'8"
Club History:	Portsmouth Barnsley
Honours/Caps:	Caps for Jamaica

In 1997, Deon Burton made his move into the Premiership when Derby County paid £1.5m for the quick-paced striker.

At the same time, he was playing an integral role with Jamaica's national squad as they battled for World Cup qualification. In September 1997, the Reggae Boyz eked out crucial one-goal wins against Canada and Costa Rica with Burton the goal-scorer in both matches. His vital contribution ensured that Jamaica reached France 98.

In February 1998, Burton was voted Jamaica's Sports Personality of the Year for his role in helping Jamaica reach the World Cup Finals. However, Deon has struggled to get into the Derby side consistently and has been out on loan during the 1998/99 season.

Darren Byfield

ASTON VILLA

Forward

Nationality:	English
Place of Birth:	Birmingham
Date of Birth:	29 September 1976
Height:	5'11"

Danny Cadamarteri

EVERTON

Forward

Nationality:	English
Place of Birth:	Bradford
Date of Birth:	12 October 1979
Height:	5'7"
Honours/Caps:	England Under 21

Kwesi Cains

STOKE CITY

Midfielder

Nationality:	English
Place of Birth:	London
Date of Birth:	5 August 1979
Height:	5'5"

Sol Campbell

TOTTENHAM HOTSPUR

Defender

Nationality:	English
Place of Birth:	London
Date of Birth:	18 September 1974
Height:	6'2"
Honours/Caps:	Full Caps for England

There have been many dynamic youngsters coming through various clubs in the Premiership, but few can claim to have made an impact on a par with Sol Campbell.

While the wranglings in the boardroom and changing rooms at Spurs have served to undermine the team's overall performance, Campbell has remained solid in a much beleaguered defence.

His game is based on composure, assurance and athleticism, and his innate ability and maturity to read the game belies his age.

Campbell's faultless performances during France 98 has definitely added to his reputation and his transfer value. He was level-headed and kept his wits about him when faced with some of the world's best strikers.

When asked about the possibility of coming up against Brazil's Ronaldo, he remarked: "It's like doing an exam. You have to study him and do the hard work and when the exam comes you know what to do."

Unfortunately, the two were never to meet in on-field combat, but one thing is certain, Sol Campbell would not have been a pushover.

Sol Campbell

Dean Canonville

MILLWALL

Forward

Nationality: English
Place of Birth: London
Date of Birth: 30 November 1978
Height: 6'1"

Martin Carruthers

PETERBOROUGH UNITED

Forward

Nationality: English
Place of Birth: Nottingham
Date of Birth: 7 August 1972
Height: 5'11"
Club History: Aston Villa
Hull City
Stoke City

Ken Charlery

BARNET

Forward

Nationality: English
Place of Birth: London
Date of Birth: 28 November 1964
Height: 6'1"
Club History: Maidstone
Peterborough United
Watford
Birmingham City
Southend
Stockport County

Lee Charles

QUEENS PARK RANGERS

Forward

Nationality: English
Place of Birth: London
Date of Birth: 20 August 1971
Height: 5'11"
Club History: Cambridge
Barnet

Iyseden Christie

MANSFIELD TOWN

Midfielder

Nationality: English
Place of Birth: Coventry
Date of Birth: 14 November 1976
Height: 6'0"
Club History: Coventry City
Bournemouth

Andy Clarke

WIMBLEDON

Forward

Nationality: English
Place of Birth: London
Date of Birth: 22 July 1967
Height: 5'10"
Club History: Barnet

Andy Clarke joined Wimbledon from Barnet in February 1991 for a modest £250,000.
While at the Hertfordshire club he scored just 17 times in 156 league appearances.
Since his transfer, he has been in and out of the Crazy Gang's first team without being able to hold down a regular place.
With the recent acquisition of some very gifted young strikers, Clarke has had few opportunities to shine at the south London club, and has spent time on loan to other clubs.

Andy Cole

Stan Collymore, left, and Des Walker

Andy Cole

MANCHESTER UNITED

Forward

Nationality: English
Place of Birth: Nottingham
Date of Birth: 15 October 1971
Height: 5'11"
Club History: Arsenal
Fulham
Bristol City
Newcastle United
Honours/Caps: FA Cup 1996 with Manchester United
Premiership 1996 and 1997 with Manchester United
Caps for England

The night that England drew with Italy to qualify for France 98, Andy Cole was missing from Glen Hoddle's line-up. Although he continued to perform solidly and consistently for Manchester United throughout the months leading up to France 98, Cole failed to make the final 22 for Hoddle's bid for World Cup glory.

Cole started his career with Arsenal but made just one appearance before he was released. Cole went on to forge a reputation for prolific goal-scoring, breaking club records at both Bristol City and Newcastle United, showing an intelligence and flair that compensated for his lack of physical presence. Alex Ferguson was encouraged enough to break the then club record to secure Cole's services for Manchester United in January 1995.

Despite breaking the Premiership scoring record with five goals in one barnstorming game against Ipswich, Cole was targeted by a succession of experts as the 'weakness' in United's side. Nevertheless, they went on to achieve a League and FA Cup Double (in 1996) and a further Premiership title (in 1997) with Cole as a prominent feature of the side.

Little mention was made of the fact that Cole had been forced to undergo a career-threatening operation on shin splints which would have upset his finely tuned balance, hair-spring reflexes and slide rule target play; the ice-cool hit man was even forced to undergo further convalescence after breaking both legs in a reserve team game during his long delayed comeback.

Cole's perseverance paid off as he returned to claim the United number nine shirt and made himself a Stretford End favourite by becoming the most consistent and prolific goal-scorer (on per game average) in United's history.

Wayne Collins

FULHAM

Midfielder

Nationality: English
Place of Birth: Manchester
Date of Birth: 4 March 1969
Height: 6'0"
Club History: Crewe Alexandra
Sheffield Wednesday

Stan Collymore

ASTON VILLA

Forward

Nationality: English
Place of Birth: Stone
Date of Birth: 22 January 1971
Height: 6'3"
Club History: Wolverhampton Wanderers
Crystal Palace
Southend United
Nottingham Forest
Liverpool
Honours/Caps: Caps for England

Stan Collymore's off-field antics have often been as well documented as his on-field endeavours. But just what is the truth behind this supremely gifted footballer?

There are no doubts about his playing ability... apart from his one goal in twenty appearances for Crystal Palace. At all the other clubs that have employed his services, he has scored goals with pleasing regularity.

It was while at Southend United, under the equally charismatic Barry Fry, that Stan Collymore began to hit the headlines. But Stan definitively became 'The Man' at Nottingham Forest, with a goal tally of 41 in just 65 games. It

was this superb record that led to his £8.5m move to Liverpool in July 1995.
However, what started off as a marriage made in heaven, turned to acrimonious divorce less than two years later. With a combination of Collymore's stubbornness and the inability of Liverpool boss, Roy Evans to harness the headstrong player, Stan was off-loaded to Aston Villa for a more than healthy £7m in May 1997.
The start of the 1997/98 season was not good for Collymore. His confidence had taken a battering and he was experiencing a severe goals drought. Coupled with his relationship with a high-profile TV personality and brushes with the law, the press - both sporting and 'secular' - had a field-day.
With a new manager at Aston Villa, Collymore has a chance to wipe the slate clean and show admirers and critics alike what he really can do. A fit, enthusiastic and clear-headed Collymore should be guaranteed a first team place and a near automatic England selection. But if the seemingly self-destructive tendencies that appear to plague him are not resolved, it may take a miracle to wake the sleeping giant.

Carl Cort

WIMBLEDON

Forward

Nationality:	English
Place of Birth:	London
Date of Birth:	1 November 1977
Height:	6'4"
Club History:	Lincoln City
Honours/Caps:	England Under-21

Carl Cort is one of a surfeit of strikers at Wimbledon. The England Under-21 player has been overshadowed by the likes of colleague Jason Euell, and his place threatened by the club's acquisition of £7.5m John Hartson - but the six-footer has the ability to harness his talent.

Ian Cox

AFC BOURNEMOUTH

Forward

Nationality:	English
Place of Birth:	Croydon
Date of Birth:	25 March 1971
Height:	6'0"
Club History:	Crystal Palace

Harvey Cunningham

DONCASTER ROVERS

Defender

Nationality:	English
Place of Birth:	Manchester
Date of Birth:	11 September 1968
Height:	5'9"

Keith Curle

WOLVERHAMPTON WANDERERS

Defender

Nationality:	English
Place of Birth:	Bristol
Date of Birth:	14 November 1963
Height:	6'0"
Club History:	Bristol Rovers
	Torquay United
	Bristol City
	Reading
	Wimbledon
	Manchester City
Honours/Caps:	Full Caps for England

Keith Curle played for a handful of clubs during his formative years, but it wasn't until he arrived at Wimbledon that he made a name for himself.
His pace and ability to read the game earned him a fine reputation, and Curle soon attracted the attentions of Manchester City. His imminent transfer caused a stir back in 1991 when City agreed a figure of £2.5m - a record-breaking sum to pay for a defender in those days.
He played for England on three occasions while at the Manchester club, and in 1996 he moved to Wolves.

Carl Cort

Andrew Cyrus

EXETER CITY

Defender

Nationality: English
Place of Birth: London
Date of Birth: 30 September 1976
Height: 5'8"
Club History: Crystal Palace

Nelson Da Costa

STOCKPORT COUNTY

Midfielder

Nationality: Portuguese
Place of Birth: Portugal
Date of Birth: 4 November 1973
Height: 6'1"
Club History: Benfica
Stoke City

Martin Dahlin

BLACKBURN ROVERS

Forward

Nationality: Swedish
Place of Birth: Sweden
Date of Birth: 16 April 1968
Height: 6'1"
Club History: A S Roma
Malmo
Honours/Caps: Caps for Sweden

Martin Dahlin made a name for himself with Sweden at the 1994 World Cup Finals in the United States. His nation finished third in the tournament and his prolific marksmanship ensured his contribution to the national side's performances did not go unnoticed.
Blackburn Rovers boss, Roy Hodgson bought Dahlin for £2.5m from Roma in July 1997, in what was another acquisition of international talent for the Premiership.
However, after a modest start with Rovers, Dahlin's first season was to be rocked by injury, and later he was unable to secure a first team place because his new boss was, understandably, reluctant to disrupt what already existed as a winning formula.

Tony Daley

WATFORD

Forward

Nationality: English
Place of Birth: Birmingham
Date of Birth: 18 October 1967
Height: 5'8"
Club History: Aston Villa
Wolverhampton Wanderers
Honours/Caps: League Cup 1994 with Aston Villa
Caps for England

Birmingham-born Tony Daley burst onto the football scene with local club, Aston Villa in 1985. He made 290 league and cup appearances for his club and saw them through to League Cup victory in 1994.
During his time at Villa, the speedy winger progressed further and he made seven appearances for England. But the dream was to turn into a nightmare when he sustained an injury which almost ended his career.
Following a spell at Wolves, Daley's career was revived when his former mentor, ex-England boss Graham Taylor took him to Watford on the eve of the 1998/99 season.

Kori Davis

NORWICH CITY

Midfielder

Nationality: German
Place of Birth: Germany
Date of Birth: 19 February 1979
Height: 6'0"
Club History: Wegberg

Martin Dahlin

Tony Daley

Marcel Desailly and Oldham's Steve Whitehall grapple for possession

Brian Deane

MIDDLESBROUGH

Forward

Nationality: British
Place of Birth: Leeds
Date of Birth: 7 February 1968
Height: 6'3"
Club History: Doncaster Rovers
Sheffield United
Leeds United

The experienced Brian Deane has, quite literally, seen and done it all. Seemingly lost to the English game after a transfer to Portuguese club Benfica, Deane made a shock return to the Premiership with a move to resurgent Middlesbrough.

His guile has been instrumental to the club's best big time form for ages and his experience undoubtedly hastened the development of fellow striker Hamilton Ricard.

Deane's major strength - and the reasons why many a manager have sought him - is primarily for his prodigious aerial ability, although he is far from limited. If Boro are to continue to progress, Deane's contribution will be vital.

Kevin Dennis

BRENTFORD

Forward

Nationality: English
Place of Birth: London
Date of Birth: 14 December 1976
Height: 5'10"
Club History: Arsenal

Marcel Desailly

CHELSEA

Defender/Midfielder

Nationality: French
Place of Birth: Accra, Ghana
Date of Birth: 7 September 1968
Height: 6'1"
Club History: Nantes
Marseilles
AC Milan
Honours/Caps: World Cup Winner 1998
European Cup with Marseilles
Caps for France

Marcel Desailly's CV makes impressive reading. The defender/midfielder has won honours at all levels since his six-year spell with first club, Nantes. Since then he has gone on to prove his class in France, Italy and now England.

Nicknamed "The Rock", Desailly's build means that there are few attackers who relish the thought of playing against him.

The only blot on a distinguished career was his sending off against Brazil during the World Cup Final in France in 1998. Even so, the winners' medal he received later that evening probably took the sting out of his 'early bath'.

Miguel DeSouza

PETERBOROUGH UNITED

Forward

Nationality: English
Place of Birth: London
Date of Birth: 11 February 1970
Height: 5'11"
Club History: Charlton Athletic
Bristol City
Birmingham City
Bury
Wycombe Wanderers

Michael Duberry

Dion Dublin

Louie Donowa

WALSALL

Forward

Nationality:	English
Place of Birth:	Ipswich
Date of Birth:	24 September 1964
Height:	5'9"
Club History:	Norwich City Stoke City Real Deportivo Helsingborgs Ipswich Town Bristol City Birmingham City Burnley Shrewsbury Town Peterborough United

Stuart Douglas

LUTON TOWN

Forward

Nationality:	English
Place of Birth:	London
Date of Birth:	9 April 1978
Height:	5'9"

Jason Dozzell

NORTHAMPTON TOWN

Midfielder

Nationality:	English
Place of Birth:	Ipswich
Date of Birth:	9 December 1967
Height:	6'1"
Club History:	Ipswich Town Tottenham Hotspur

Michael Duberry

CHELSEA

Defender

Nationality:	English
Place of Birth:	Enfield, Middlesex
Date of Birth:	14 October 1975
Height:	6'1"
Club History:	Bournemouth
Honours/Caps:	League Cup in 1998 with Chelsea European Cup Winners' Cup in 1998 with Chelsea Caps for England Under 21s

Dubbed as one of the best English centre-backs to have emerged in recent years, Michael Duberry's progress has not always matched predictions.

His appearances for the Blues have been hampered by injuries and the success of team-mates Marcel Desailly and Frank Lebeouf who have created an effective partnership at Chelsea.

Dion Dublin

ASTON VILLA

Forward

Nationality:	English
Place of Birth:	Leicester
Date of Birth:	22 April 1969
Height:	6'2"
Club History:	Norwich City Cambridge United Manchester United Coventry
Honours/Caps:	Third Division Championship 1991 with Cambridge United Caps for England

Dion Dublin gained a healthy reputation during 152 appearances for Cambridge United. But the big time beckoned in the shape of Alex Ferguson and the mighty Manchester United.

However, his move to one of England's top clubs was short-lived. After making only a dozen appearances, he sustained a broken leg which subsequently ended his time at United.

Coventry City rescued him from his Manchester disappointment and the Sky Blues of Highfield

Kieron Dyer

Bruce Dyer in the thick of it at Crystal Palace

Road more than had their money's worth from the multi-talented player. During the 1998/99 season Aston Villa bought him for £5.75m and he is, once again, proving to be a bargain.
Dublin has proved that apart from being able to poach a goal or two, he also has the ability to stop them as well. In most matches, the industrious Dublin can be seen skippering his team-mates by example in both the opposition as well as his own penalty-box.
One of the highlights in his career came when he made his debut for England against Chile in February 1998. Although he did not make the England squad for the World Cup, England coach Glenn Hoddle publicly stated that one of his hardest deliberations led to him leaving Dublin out of the squad.

Keith Dublin

SOUTHEND UNITED

Defender

Nationality: English
Place of Birth: High Wycombe
Date of Birth: 29 January 1966
Height: 6'0"
Club History: Chelsea
Brighton & Hove Albion
Watford

Bruce Dyer

BARNSLEY

Forward

Nationality: English
Place of Birth: Ilford, Essex
Date of Birth: 13 April 1975
Height: 6'0"
Club History: Watford
Crystal Palace
Honours/Caps: First Division Championship 1994 with Crystal Palace
Caps for England Under 21s

Bruce Dyer was a £1.1m purchase from Watford in March 1994, making him, at the time, the most expensive teenager in Britain. He played 38 times for Watford where he scored nine goals. Like so many players, Dyer has the potential, but he needs to add consistency to his game if he is to become a major player.

Kieron Dyer

IPSWICH TOWN

Defender

Nationality: English
Place of Birth: Ipswich
Date of Birth: 29 December 1978
Height: 5'7"
Honours/Caps: Caps for England Youth and England Under 21s

Arsenal were mooted to be the latest big club to be showing an interest in the multi-talented Kieron Dyer. The England Youth international is set for a glittering career; it's just a case of when and where. Ipswich have made it quite clear that if anyone is going to prise their biggest asset away from Portman Road they should be prepared to start negotiations with £4m.

Robbie Earle

WIMBLEDON

Midfielder

Nationality: English
Place of Birth: Newcastle-under-Lyme
Date of Birth: 27 January 1965
Height: 5'9"
Club History: Port Vale
Honours/Caps: Caps for Jamaica

The world stage of France 98 deserved to see a player of Robbie Earle's class. After all, it is Earle who brings calm assurance to the hurly-burly of his club's Premiership displays.
Having played 294 times for humble Port Vale, it is to his own credit that Robbie Earle has matured into a player of immense class. This maturity has earned him the captaincy at the south London club since the departure of Vinny Jones.
The same respect has also been accorded him on the international stage. Just when the English

Robbie Earle

media was cajoling Terry Venables and then Glenn Hoddle to give the Wimbledon midfielder his England debut, Earle chose to exercise his option of playing for Jamaica.
Jamaica's qualification owed much to Robbie Earle. Although the Reggae Boyz are a potent mix of home-grown talent and those plying their trade in the Premier and Football League, it was Earle's experience and maturity that provided a major factor in the Caribbean side's qualification to France 98.
"The hard work starts now," he said. "That's why it is essential that we go to France with the intention to achieve something and not just with the thought of having a good time."
Earle scored Jamaica's first ever World Cup goal against Croatia in France 98.

Ugo Ehiogu

ASTON VILLA

Defender

Nationality:	English
Place of Birth:	London
Date of Birth:	3 November 1972
Height:	6'2"
Club History:	West Bromwich Albion
Honours/Caps:	League Cup 1996 with Aston Villa Caps for England

Ugo Ehiogu has worn an England shirt at full and Under-21 level on several occasions since his debut in 1992.
Apart from his junior England honours, Ehiogu has tasted success in the Football League Cup, a trophy in which Villa have always traditionally done well.
Having joined West Bromwich Albion as a trainee he made just two appearances for them before he joined the self-appointed 'pride of the Midlands', Aston Villa.

Efan Ekoku

WIMBLEDON

Forward

Nationality:	English
Place of Birth:	Manchester
Date of Birth:	8 June 1967
Height:	6'1"
Club History:	Bournemouth Norwich City
Honours/Caps:	Caps for Nigeria

Nicknamed 'Chief' by team-mates, Efan Ekoku is a Nigerian international player who was born in Manchester and made his English debut with non-league Sutton United.
Since those humble beginnings, the big man has gone on to take further journeys in his nomadic career. In May 1990 he signed a professional contract with Bournemouth and almost three years later he moved on to Norwich.
Now, he is the attacking focal point for the Premiership's most unfashionable club, and like his team-mates, he is adept at unsettling the Premiership's finest defenders.
Ekoku bears more than a striking resemblance, in looks and style of play, to the former Wimbledon icon, John Fashanu. Like Fashanu, Ekoku has a multitude of ball skills is a real handful in terms of his strength and pace. However, his forte is being a constant aerial threat to opponents.

Lee Ellington

HULL CITY

Midfielder

Nationality:	English
Place of Birth:	Bradford
Date of Birth:	3 July 1980
Height:	5'10"

Ugo Ehiogu

Jason Euell, left, and Derby's Daryll Powell

Efan Ekoku

Jason Euell

WIMBLEDON

Forward

Nationality:	English
Place of Birth:	London
Date of Birth:	6 February 1977
Height:	6'0"
Honours/Caps:	England Under 21

Wimbledon have gained a reputation for nurturing young talent and then making huge profits by selling them on. Jason Euell could be the next starlet to come off the conveyer belt.
His ability to play up front or midfield makes him a prodigious talent with a big future. Manager Joe Kinnear rates Euell highly as does club captain Robbie Earle, who believes that with continued application and attitude "it is just a matter of time" before his team-mate hits the big time.

Scott Eustace

MANSFIELD TOWN

Forward

Nationality:English

Place of Birth:	Leicester
Date of Birth:	13 June 1975
Height:	6'0"
Club History:	Leicester City

Delroy Facey

HUDDERSFIELD TOWN

Forward

Nationality:	English
Place of Birth:	Huddersfield
Date of Birth:	22 April 1980
Height:	6'0"

Chris Fairclough

NOTTS COUNTY

Defender

Nationality:	English
Place of Birth:	Nottingham
Date of Birth:	12 April 1964
Height:	5'11"
Club History:	Nottingham Forest Tottenham Hotspur Leeds United Bolton Wanderers
Honours/Caps:	First Division Championship 1992 with Leeds United and 1997 with Bolton Wanderers Caps for England

It could be said that Chris Fairclough has seen and done it all in his 17-year professional career. It was at his home town club, Nottingham Forest, that this athletic centre-half was to emerge.
Under the guidance of Brian Clough, Fairclough put in noteworthy displays time and time again as Forest upset the big guns. In 1987, after a six-year career with Forest, Tottenham Hotspur were to invest in Fairclough's skills for what was, at the time, a considerable sum - £387,000.
At Tottenham, Fairclough was to continue to win rave reviews, but surprisingly only one England B cap. But he eventually received his just reward as a member of the Leeds United side which won the First Division Championship in 1992. He had joined the team three years earlier for £500,000 and had formed a gritty and instrumental centre-half partnership with Chris Whyte.
However, at Bolton, and during the team's one and only season in the Premiership, Fairclough was unable to hold down a first team place, with manager Colin Todd seemingly compelled to beef-up his squad with new purchases.

Les Ferdinand

TOTTENHAM HOTSPUR

Forward

Nationality:	English
Place of Birth:	London
Date of Birth:	18 December 1966
Height:	5'11"
Club History:	Queens Park Rangers Brentford Besiktas Newcastle United
Honours/Caps:	Turkish FA Cup 1989 with Besiktas Caps for England

It was once suggested that Les Ferdinand would partner the awesomely talented Alan Shearer on a regular basis on the international playing fields. As things stood, six months before the 1998 World Cup in France, 'Sir Les' - the regal title of his autobiography - looked like he might struggle to make Glenn Hoddle's France 98 squad. He made the squad, however, but did not make the team.

Injury and loss of form have seen the former darling of Queens Park Rangers plummet in the highly competitive race to partner Shearer as England's cutting edge.

In the blue and white hoops of Rangers, Ferdinand scored almost a goal every other game with 80 goals in 163 appearances. But it was not all plain sailing for this lover of fine clothes and expensive watches. He had two loan spells while with the west London outfit. Firstly, his talents took him to nearby Brentford and that three-game spell was followed by a stint in Turkey with Besiktas.

Ferdinand's quick feet, second-to-none heading ability and bustling determination saw him play 24 times for the Turkish side and hit the back of the net 14 times.

It was that Eastern promise that saw him return to Rangers with credentials enhanced. Big clubs at home and abroad were now sitting up and taking notice of a player who always had the potential but had never shown it consistently.

The big man went on to be consistent and landed himself a lucrative move to Newcastle United, home to possibly the most passionate set of supporters in England. On his arrival Ferdinand did much to ease the pain the Geordies had suffered when their former idol, Andy Cole, was sold suddenly to arch rivals Manchester United. Ferdinand found his Rangers form to ensure that Cole was not missed too much.

But his problems began to mount when, with the Cole money, Newcastle bought Shearer, the best player of his type in Britain. Part of Shearer's deal was that he would wear/claim the coveted No. 9 shirt which, up until then, had been the property of Ferdinand. Naturally, he was not happy and from there his relationship with then boss Kevin Keegan slowly, but surely, went downhill.

Once Keegan had moved on, a fresh start was anticipated - in the shape of Kenny Dalglish. After the shirt debacle, Ferdinand was to be at the centre of another shock - the club were prepared to sell him due, allegedly, to the demands of the money men, who are increasingly playing a dominant role in modern football's wheelings and dealings.

So, Ferdinand was on his way, returning to the south of England to a new home, this time the north London outfit, Tottenham, for a cool £6m. Injury was to see him lose his place in the team and just to make matters worse, Spurs' chairman presented the fans with an enthusiastically received 1997 Christmas present with the purchase of Germany's World Cup captain and striker, Jurgen Klinsmann, to boost a much maligned Tottenham strike force.

All in all, Ferdinand's move to Spurs, to date, has not been an unqualified success. There was even talk at the start of the World Cup year that the man who once delighted fans in Turkish grounds may be off-loaded. It's a funny old game!

Les Ferdinand

Les Ferdinand battling with Everton's Craig Short

Rio Ferdinand

Rio Ferdinand

WEST HAM UNITED

Defender

Nationality:	English
Place of Birth:	London
Date of Birth:	7 November 1978
Height:	6'2"
Club History:	Bournemouth
Honours/Caps:	Two Caps for England

A resounding sigh of relief reverberated around the East End of London on 16 December 1997, the day that West Ham United secured the long term future of their stylish defender Rio Ferdinand.

Rio - second cousin to Tottenham Hotspur's Les - signed a lucrative seven-year contract that will, hopefully, keep him at Upton Park until 2005. West Ham's chief executive, Peter Storrie, summed up the club's and the fans' feeling when he said directly after the deal had been done: "We are absolutely delighted to conclude the contract with Rio."

So what a start it has been for Ferdinand, who has already been dubbed the next Bobby Moore by the older generation of the Upton Park faithful.

All good footballers make the ball work for them. The really great footballers make time for themselves and Ferdinand is in the latter category. For one so young he reads the game impressively. In fact, his skill is such that he makes experienced strikers look quite ordinary at times.

Rio is a rare talent. South London-born, he made his full England debut against Cameroon in November 1997 and gave an impressive performance.

To date, John Barnes is the most capped Black player with over seventy caps. Provided Rio lives up to his potential, there is no doubt he can achieve one hundred international caps.

A place in England's squad for France 98 was his reward for an outstanding season in 1997/98. He is still prone to the odd, costly simple mistake and the best thing that his coaches, presently Harry Redknapp and Glenn Hoddle, can do for him is give him some more time to develop.

Richard Flash

WATFORD

Midfielder

Nationality:	English
Place of Birth:	Birmingham
Date of Birth:	8 April 1976
Height:	5'9"
Club History:	Manchester United

Curtis Fleming

MIDDLESBROUGH

Defender

Nationality:	English
Place of Birth:	Manchester
Date of Birth:	8 October 1968
Height:	5'8"
Club History:	St Patrick's
Honours/Caps:	First Division Championship 1990 with Middlesbrough Eight Caps for Ireland

Since the start of his Boro career in 1991, Chris Fleming has been a regular figure in the club's topsy-turvy recent history. He was in the Boro team that lost two Cup finals - the Coca Cola Cup to Leicester City and the FA Cup to Chelsea - in one, miserable 1996/97 season. To compound the misery for Fleming and Co. the club was also relegated in the same season. Fleming, an Eire international, then found that his, and the club's, first season back in the First Division no better than the previous one, as an appendix operation put him out of action for months. However, the season ended on a happier note as Middlesbrough, with Fleming in their ranks, won promotion to the Premiership in 1998.

Curtis Fleming

Marc Vivien Foe

Jimmy Floyd-Hasselbaink

Terry Fleming

LINCOLN CITY

Midfielder

Nationality: English
Place of Birth: West Midlands
Date of Birth: 5 January 1973
Height: 5'9"
Club History: Coventry City
Northampton Town
Preston North End

Jimmy Floyd-Hasselbaink

LEEDS UNITED

Forward

Nationality: Dutch
Place of Birth: Surinam
Date of Birth: 27 March 1972
Height: 5'10"
Club History: Boavista
Honours/Caps: Four Caps for Holland

The 1997/98 season was a tremendous one for Premiership newcomer Jimmy Floyd-Hasselbaink. Signed by George Graham early in his new management post at Leeds, Hasselbaink was a relative unknown to football fans in England. However, by the end of the season he had made his mark with more than twenty goals and his now trademark cartwheel celebration.

His top form for the Yorkshire club gained him a call-up for Holland's World Cup squad, but the return from injury of Dennis Bergkamp denied him further starting opportunities. There is no doubt that a long international career awaits this prolific goal-scorer.

Marc Vivien Foe

WEST HAM UNITED

Midfielder

Nationality: Cameroonian
Place of Birth: Cameroon
Date of Birth: 1 May 1975
Height: 5'7"
Club History: Lens
Honours/Caps: Caps for Cameroon

Marc Vivien Foe was acquired by West Ham United in January 1999. Originally destined for Manchester United, Foe suffered a broken leg towards the end of 1998 which put paid to any chances of signing for the Red devils.

Adrian Forbes

NORWICH CITY

Forward

Nationality: English
Place of Birth: London
Date of Birth: 23 January 1979
Height: 5'7"
Honours/Caps: Caps for England Youth

Adrian Forbes is an England Youth International who possesses exciting goal-scoring potential which should see him hit the same heights as former Norwich City strikers, the Fashanu brothers and Efan Ekoku.

Steven Forbes

COLCHESTER UNITED

Midfielder

Nationality: English
Place of Birth: London
Date of Birth: 24 December 1975
Height: 6'2"
Club History: Sittingbourne
Millwall

Tony Ford

MANSFIELD TOWN

Midfielder

Nationality: English
Place of Birth: Grimsby, Lincolnshire
Date of Birth: 14 May 1959
Height: 5'9"
Club History: Grimsby Town
Stoke City
Sunderland
West Bromwich Albion
Bradford City
Scunthorpe United

With 825 appearances (at the time of going to press), Tony Ford broke the League record for appearances.

Ruel Fox

TOTTENHAM HOTSPUR

Forward

Nationality: English
Place of Birth: Ipswich
Date of Birth: 14 January 1968
Height: 5'6"
Club History: Norwich City
Newcastle United
Honours/Caps: Two Caps for England B

Like so many before him, Ruel Fox was a product of Norwich City, for so long a conveyor belt of talent from the East.
Having produced the newsworthy Fashanu brothers, Justin and John, Fox kept up the very finest of Norwich traditions by proving to be a fleet-footed diamond. Like so many of Norwich's young talent, Fox was to be lured by the bright lights of a big city club, Newcastle United.
He was to become part of 'King' Kevin Keegan's renaissance in the North East. It could not have been more of a contrast to the rural setting of homely Norwich.
Following an initial and dramatic impact in the black and white stripes of United, Fox was to lose his place in the first team - his exciting forays made in the green and yellow of Norwich were never quite duplicated under Keegan.
Fox moved on to Tottenham Hotspur who paid £4.5m for his services but, once again, this has not proved to be the perfect setting for the Suffolk-born lad.
His international ambitions as well as his quest for domestic honours - two things he was looking to enhance when he left Norwich - are in danger of being unfulfilled if the form of his youth does not reappear.

Kevin Francis

OXFORD UNITED

Forward

Nationality: English
Place of Birth: Birmingham
Date of Birth: 6 December 1967
Height: 6'7"
Club History: Mile Oak Rovers
Derby County
Stockport County
Birmingham City

Chris Freestone

NORTHAMPTON TOWN

Forward

Nationality: English
Place of Birth: Nottingham
Date of Birth: 4 September 1971
Height: 5'11"
Club History: Arnold
Carlisle united
Middlesbrough

Paul Furlong

BIRMINGHAM CITY

Forward

Nationality: English
Place of Birth: London
Date of Birth: 1 October 1968
Height: 6'0"
Club History: Enfield Town
Coventry City
Watford
Chelsea

When Birmingham City made Paul Furlong their record transfer, in a move from Chelsea for £1.5m in July 1996, they bought one of the Division's most experienced marksmen.

His goal-scoring ability first appeared while at Coventry City. From there he moved to Watford for £250,000 in 1992 where he attracted much attention with his direct, bustling style of play. Chelsea were to invest in his potential when they snapped him up for £2.3m in May 1994. Alas, his move into the big time never really took off. He made just 80 appearances with a goals return of just 17 before Birmingham City boss, Trevor Francis ended his spell in London.

Ricardo Gardner

BOLTON WANDERERS

Midfield/Forward

Nationality: Jamaican
Place of Birth: Jamaica
Height: 5'10"
Club History: Harbour View, Jamaica
Honours/Caps: Full Caps for Jamaica

After the exposure of the World Cup in France, Ricardo Gardner was the first of the Reggae Boyz to be snapped up by an English football league club. Bolton Wanderers boss Colin Todd had seen enough of the winger during France 98 to capture his signature.

Gardner is full of tricks and nimble footwork but to date he is not a first team choice for the Lancashire club. Like many newcomers to the League, it looks like it will take the youngster some time to adjust to the rigours of the English game which requires continual effort as well as football ability.

John Gayle

NORTHAMPTON TOWN

Forward

Nationality: English
Place of Birth: Bromsgrove
Date of Birth: 30 July 1964
Height: 6'4"
Club History: Burton Albion
Wimbledon
Birmingham City
Walsall
Coventry City
Burnley
Stoke City
Gillingham

Marcus Gayle

WIMBLEDON

Forward

Nationality: English
Place of Birth: London
Date of Birth: 27 September 1970
Height: 6'1"
Club History: Brentford
Honours/Caps: Third Division Championship
1992 with Brentford
Five Caps for Jamaica

West Londoner, Marcus Gayle was faced with a dilemma of international proportions. Invited by Jamaica to be part of their squad for the World Cup in 1998, his impressive form was garnering attention from England coach Glenn Hoddle. The decision to opt for the Reggae Boyz was made after much soul searching. However, the problems did not end there, as Wimbledon claimed he would not miss Premiership matches if he was playing for England. The matter was resolved when FIFA ruled Gayle must be released and allowed to play for Jamaica. In February 1998, he made his debut and helped the Reggae Boyz to achieve,

Paul Furlong

Marcus Gayle

arguably, the best result in their history - a draw with then World Champions Brazil. The hard running powerful forward, who has thrived in a very underrated Wimbledon side, made the Jamaican World Cup '98 squad.

Mark Gayle

CREWE ALEXANDRA

Goalkeeper

Nationality: English
Place of Birth: Bromsgrove, Tyne & Wear
Date of Birth: 21 October 1969
Height: 6'2"
Club History: Leicester City
Blackpool
Worcester City
Walsall

Liam George

LUTON TOWN

Forward

Nationality: English
Place of Birth: Luton
Date of Birth: 2 February 1979
Height: 5'10"

Earl Gilkes

WOLVERHAMPTON WANDERERS

Forward

Nationality: English
Place of Birth: London
Date of Birth: 20 July 1965
Height: 5'8"
Club History: Leicester City
Reading
Chelsea
Southampton

Jon Gittens

TORQUAY UNITED

Defender

Nationality: English
Place of Birth: Birmingham
Date of Birth: 22 January 1964
Height: 5'11"
Club History: Pageant Rangers
Southampton
Swindon Town
Middlesbrough
Portsmouth

Byron Glasgow

READING

Midfielder

Nationality: English
Place of Birth: London
Date of Birth: 18 February 1979
Height: 5'6"

Shaun Goater

MANCHESTER CITY

Forward

Nationality: Bermudan
Place of Birth: Bermuda
Date of Birth: 25 February 1970
Height: 5'11"
Club History: Rotherham United
Notts County
Lambada, West Indies
Bristol City

Ty Gooden

SWINDON TOWN

Midfielder

Nationality: English
Place of Birth: Essex
Date of Birth: 23 October 1972
Height: 5'8"
Club History: Arsenal
Wycombe Wanderers

Don Goodman

BARNSLEY

Forward

Nationality: English
Place of Birth: Leeds
Date of Birth: 9 May 1966
Height: 5'1"
Club History: Collingham
Bradford City
West Bromwich Albion
Sunderland
Wolverhampton Wanders

Gregory Goodridge

BRISTOL CITY

Forward

Nationality: Barbadian
Place of Birth: Barbados
Date of Birth: 10 July 1971
Height: 5'6"
Club History: Torquay United
Queens Park Rangers

Dean Gordon

MIDDLESBROUGH

Defender

Nationality: English
Place of Birth: London
Date of Birth: 10 February 1973
Height: 6'0"
Club History: Crystal Palace
Honours/Caps: First Division Championship 1994 with Crystal Palace
13 Caps for England Under 21s

Dean Gordon signed for Crystal Palace in July 1991. A solid defender with a ferocious left foot shot, he accumulated 13 England Under-21 caps and one Division One Championship in 1994.
He was Palace's second longest serving professional and saw the club through the good times and the bad.
Gordon's versatility has seen him play in an exciting left-back or midfield position, as well as in a central defensive role. However, in July 1998, Dean Gordon ceased to be part of the team's recovery programme when he made a shock move to Middlesbrough for £1m.

Gavin Gordon

HULL CITY

Forward

Nationality: English
Place of Birth: Manchester
Date of Birth: 24 June 1979
Height: 6'1"

Warren Hackett

MANSFIELD TOWN

Defender

Nationality: English
Place of Birth: London
Date of Birth: 16 December 1971
Height: 6'0"
Club History: Tottenham Hotspur
Leyton Orient
Doncaster Rovers

Marcus Hall

COVENTRY CITY

Defender

Nationality: English
Place of Birth: Coventry
Date of Birth: 24 March 1976
Height: 6'1"
Honours/Caps: Five Caps for England Under 21s

The continued rise of defender Marcus Hall has been cobra-like - quiet but swift. Having made his debut in the 1996/97 season, Hall has already been showered with England Under-21 honours. But one of his greatest assets is the ability to remain composed when all around him are losing their heads. Much of this composure and discipline stems from an encouraging family who have backed him from the beginning.
Ossie Franks, a man with his hand very firmly

Dean Gordon fends off Igor Stimac

Marcus Hall

on Coventry's pulse, has seen the likes of Cyrille Regis and Danny Thomas don the blue shirt of his favourite club. He feels that young Hall has the ability to continue the high standards of that famous duo.

Paul Hall

COVENTRY CITY

Midfielder

Nationality:	Jamaican
Place of Birth:	Manchester
Date of Birth:	3 July 1972
Height:	5'9"
Club History:	Torquay United Portsmouth Bury
Honours/Caps:	21 Caps for Jamaica

Paul Hall is one of the unsung heroes of both club and country. He is a tireless and determined player whose contribution has been first class.

After his performance for Jamaica during the World Cup, Hall was approached by Coventry City and snapped up for the bargain price of £300,000 just before the start of the 1998/99 season.

Des Hamilton

NEWCASTLE UNITED

Midfielder

Nationality:	English
Place of Birth:	Bradford
Date of Birth:	15 August 1976
Height:	5'10"
Club History:	Bradford City, Sheffield United
Honours/Caps:	One Cap for England Under 21s

When former Newcastle boss Kenny Dalglish forked out £1.5m in March 1997 for Bradford City's Des Hamilton, many asked, "Des who?" But Dalglish, who unearthed and polished such gems as John Barnes and Steve McMannaman, knows a player when he sees one and the progress and development of Hamilton should be noted with intrigue.

During his few appearances for the Geordies, Hamilton has shown similar qualities to former United no-nonsense dynamo David Batty. Like Batty, Hamilton's goal return is poor. In 88 appearances for Bradford - the club he joined as a trainee - He found the net just five times.

Hamilton's dream move to Newcastle United has proved to be far from that. Signed by former boss Kenny Dalglish at the start of an alleged bright new era for the club, Hamilton has found himself surplus to requirements under exiting boss Ruud Gullit.

Loan spells at Sheffield United and Huddersfield Town have possibly signalled the end of his career in the north-east.

Dave Hanson

LEYTON ORIENT

Forward

Nationality:	English
Place of Birth:	Huddersfield
Date of Birth:	19 November 1968
Height:	6'1"
Club History:	Bury Chesterfield

Marlon Harewood

NOTTINGHAM FOREST

Forward

Nationality:	British
Place of Birth:	Hampstead
Date of Birth:	25 August 1979
Height:	6'1"

Paul Hall

Michael Harle

BARNET

Defender

Nationality: English
Place of Birth: London
Date of Birth: 31 October 1972
Height: 5'1"
Club History: Gillingham
Sittingbourne
Millwall
Bury

Kevin Harper

DERBY COUNTY

Forward

Nationality: English
Place of Birth: Oldham
Date of Birth: 15 January 1976
Height: 5'6"
Club History: Hibernian

Emile Heskey

LEICESTER CITY

Forward

Nationality: English
Place of Birth: Leicester
Date of Birth: 11 January 1978
Height: 6'2"
Honours/Caps: League Cup 1997 with Leicester City
Five Caps for England Under 21s

Dubbed 'Bruno' by the Leicester City faithful, Emile Heskey has all the credentials to be a real heavyweight in soccer's arena.
Heskey has all the physical attributes of his boxing namesake. He is over six-foot and weighs in at a mean 14 stone.
But Heskey's footballing attributes are more akin to Cyrille Regis, the former West Bromwich Albion and Coventry City striker. Like Regis, Heskey has electric pace, as well as an eye for goal.
Sadly for Leicester fans, they may not see the best of Heskey who has been linked to a transfer to a bigger club - possibly Liverpool - to form a little and large duo up front with Robbie Fowler or Michael Owen. This mouth-watering prospect brings back memories of Liverpool's last odd couple - John Toshack and Kevin Keegan.

Shaka Hislop

WEST HAM UNITED

Goalkeeper

Nationality: English
Place of Birth: London
Date of Birth: 22 February 1969
Height: 6'4"
Club History: Reading
Newcastle United
Honours/Caps: Second Division Championship 1994 with Reading
Two Caps for England Under 21s

Not so long ago, cynics doubted whether Black players could play anywhere apart from up front. Over a period of time that line of thinking has been banished. The advancement of Black players has seen them not only score goals but also find their niche in defence and midfield.
As yet, however, the goal-keeper's position still does not register boldly on the progress chart. Shaka Hislop is doing his best to change that. He is an excellent 'keeper at a top-class club which gains plenty of exposure.
Purchased from Reading in August 1995 for £1.5m, Hislop was a key component in former Newcastle boss Kevin Keegan's Master Plan. Hislop proved his worth not only by moving up a division (the gap between the First Division and the Premiership widens annually) but he also staved off the challenge of first-choice 'keeper Pavel Srnicek of Czechoslovakia to make the green jersey his own.
The move from Elm Park, Reading, has seen the smooth-looking Hislop elevated into the world of big-time pressure games at home and abroad. He has dealt with that new found status admirably.
Not only is he a good shot-stopper but Hislop has a lean, agile body which he throws through

Emile Heskey

Shaka Hislop

Pierre van Hooijdonk

the air with great success. He was never short of work while under Keegan's stewardship, and more recently Kenny Dalglish's. The United defence has never been noted for rock-like solidity - they are likely to score four goals a game, but concede three in doing so!

Hislop's international aspirations received a tremendous boost when he was called up to the England squad in February 1998. Born in the heart of the East End he is keen to carve out a domestic and international career. Heart is something that all footballers need, but especially goalkeepers.

Under the Bosman ruling, Hislop moved on a free transfer to West Ham United in the summer of 1998.

Pierre van Hooijdonk

NOTTINGHAM FOREST

Forward

Nationality:	Dutch
Place of Birth:	Holland
Date of Birth:	29 November 1969
Height:	6'4"
Club History:	NAC Breda Celtic
Honours/Caps:	First Division Championship 1998 with Nottingham Forest 14 Caps for Holland

Pierre van Hooijdonk is, arguably, the most controversial player in the Premiership. He was so incensed when, after being promoted from the First Division, Forest sold his prolific striking partner Kevin Campbell, he went on a one-man strike. Van Hooijdonk claimed the sale was a sign of a lack of ambition and Forest were simply not good enough to survive in the Premiership. This has proved correct as Forest look set for relegation back to First Division come May '99. His return from Holland after his 'strike' resulted in fans, the club and media condemning his behaviour. Former manager Dave Bassett even attributed one of the reasons for his sacking to the Dutch international's strike action. The Dutchman's bad boy reputation has preceded him at every club he has performed for. But the sometimes fickle nature of the sport has seen this scourge of management become the darling of the fans with his phenomenal goal-scoring record. Now a full Dutch international, van Hooijdonk made everyone sit up and take notice when he joined Scottish giants, Glasgow Celtic in January 1995 for £1.2m. In just 63 full league starts he scored 46 times. Add his nine goals in just ten cup games and you can see why his outspoken nature was quickly forgiven. His prolific scoring saw him transfer to Forest in March 1997 for a value-for-money price of £4.5m, and his goals assured Forest's promotion to the Premiership in 1998. The success of that initial season has now turned sour.

Augustus Hurdle

BRENTFORD

Defender

Nationality:	English
Place of Birth:	London
Date of Birth:	14 October 1973
Height:	5'9"
Club History:	Fulham Dorchester

Carl Hutchins

BRENTFORD

Midfielder

Nationality:	English
Place of Birth:	London
Date of Birth:	24 September 1974
Height:	5'11"

Micha Hyde

WATFORD

Defender

Nationality:	English
Place of Birth:	London
Date of Birth:	10 November 1974
Height:	5'9"
Club History:	Cambridge United

Andy Impey

LEICESTER CITY

Midfielder

Nationality:	English
Place of Birth:	London
Date of Birth:	30 September 1971
Height:	5'8"
Club History:	Yeading Queens Park Rangers West Ham United
Honours/Caps:	One Cap for England Under 21s

For such a good team player, the transfer of Andy Impey from West Ham to Leicester proved to be one of the most controversial. Strapped for cash, West Ham sold Impey for £1.2m - without the knowledge of West Ham manager Harry Redknapp, who considered the versatile England Under-21 international a vital part of his squad. Although full international honours seem far away, he is one of those players every team needs. Impey can play in a variety of positions, without seeming out of place.

Paul Ince

LIVERPOOL

Midfielder

Nationality:	English
Place of Birth:	Essex
Date of Birth:	21 October 1967
Height:	5'10"
Club History:	West Ham United Manchester United Inter Milan
Honours/Caps:	FA Cup 1990 with Manchester United European Cup Winners' Cup 1991 with Manchester United League Cup 1992 with Manchester United Premiership 1993 and 1994 with Manchester United 42 Caps for England

Not too many players have the ability to make a name for themselves at the two biggest clubs in England. However, East Ender Paul Ince is one such man having donned the red shirts of both Manchester United and, in more recent times, Liverpool.

Throw in a stint at the academy of football, West Ham United, and a spell at Italian giants, Inter Milan, and you can see that Ince is a class player with a medal haul to prove it.

Liverpool have always had a hard-tackling, ball-winning midfielder. In the recent past they have had Jimmy Case, Graeme Souness and Steve McMahon. Ince looks set to carry on the fine traditions of that trio of winners. Dubbed 'The Guvnor', even as a youngster, he certainly is the boss of his team's midfield.

His talents have also seen him captain England on an occasional basis in the absence of the likes of Tony Adams and Alan Shearer. Ince's swashbuckling play was instrumental as England so very nearly reached the Final of Euro 96. For club and country, Ince is an irresistible driving force who expects the highest standards on the field of play from himself as well as his team-mates. There has been many a time when he can be seen to be remonstrating with an opponent (or a team-mate) such is his desire to win.

Nobody should think that Ince's game stops and starts with powerful, surging runs from box to box. No, he can certainly play a bit too. Apart from breaking up opponents' forays, Ince's famed, powerful long-distance shots and ability to spray the ball to a team-mate some distance away, make him an automatic choice for both club and country.

Since his early, formative years at West Ham, Ince has matured. There was a time while at the Upton Park club when bust ups with officials and red/yellow cards were something of the norm. Even while at Manchester, he was noted for his run-ins with officialdom.

But the Italian experience seems to have been just the job for his fiery temperament. Ince, cousin to former world middleweight boxing champion Nigel Benn, will always have a cutting edge to his game. He is a bit like former team mate Eric Cantona in that respect. If you took away their natural aggression, you would take away the essence of their footballing identity.

Anyway, Ince is still far from being a pussycat.

Andy Impey

Paul Ince

Paul Ince

David James

When asked by Total Sport magazine who was the hardest player he had faced during his career, Ince answered in the manner with which we have become accustomed: "I am not being flash or clever, but I don't fear anyone. If I play my game, I know I've got no reason to fear anyone. If I play well against any opponent I'll come out on top."

Rodney Jack

CREWE ALEXANDRA

Forward

Nationality: Jamaican
Place of Birth: Jamaica
Date of Birth: 28 September 1972
Height: 5'7"
Club History: Lambada, West Indies
Torquay United

David James

LIVERPOOL

Goalkeeper

Nationality: English
Place of Birth: Watford
Date of Birth: 1 August 1970
Height: 6'5"
Club History: Watford
Honours/Caps: League Cup 1995 with Liverpool
One Cap for England

Hertfordshire-born David James was to be the second successful Watford man to move to Liverpool, following in the footsteps of John Barnes. James played 89 times for Elton John's favourite club.

At the start of his Anfield career in July 1992, James had quite an act to follow. After all, the Anfielders were used to the likes of England's Ray Clemence and the zany, but talented Zimbabwean, Bruce Grobbelar.

After an impressive start to his Liverpool career, in recent seasons James has been subjected to microscopic like scrutiny, due to some of the errors he has made in big games. Indeed, his future seemed to lie away from the club, following the purchase of American international Brad Freidel. But then joint-managers, Roy Evans and Gerad Houllier kept faith with James and the player himself has been a model professional in his time of crisis.

Talking of model, James' looks have allowed him to earn an income away from the field of play. He dyed his hair blond to appear on the front cover of Arena magazine and has modelled underwear for Armani.

Married with two children, James has been one of several Liverpool players dubbed 'The Spice Boys' such has been their laid back approach and under-achievement. In response to the snipers he told Match of the Day: "That Spice Boys thing is crap. We're not a gang of rowdy chums who all go down to the pub together."

In February 1998, James was to lose the 'keeper's jersey to Freidel after 212 consecutive performances for the club spanning four years. However, hard work, allied with consistent form in the reserve team, has led to a return to the first team.

Tony James

PLYMOUTH ARGYLE

Defender

Nationality: English
Place of Birth: Sheffield
Date of Birth: 27 June 1967
Height: 6'3"
Club History: Gainsborough Town
Lincoln City
Leicester City
Hereford United

Earl Jean

PLYMOUTH ARGYLE

Forward

Nationality: English
Place of Birth: St Lucia
Date of Birth: 9 October 1971
Height: 5'8"
Club History: Ipswich Town
Rotherham United

Julian Joachim

Julian Joachim

ASTON VILLA

Forward

Nationality:	English
Place of Birth:	Peterborough
Date of Birth:	20 September 1974
Height:	5'6"
Club History:	Leicester City
Honours/Caps:	Nine Caps for England Under 21s

Just a few years ago Julian Joachim had a £4m price tag on his head and he looked set to collect honours both domestically and internationally. To date, that promise has yet to materialise.

Leicester City were the first to put their faith in the promise of Joachim, and it was there that he was to earn rave reviews. In 92 league and cup appearances, he scored 29 times. The stocky forward has pace and the ability to run menacingly and directly at opponents. Leicester's assistant manager, Alan Evans, summed up his talents: "It's not just his speed. He can move the ball quickly from foot to foot or he can knock it into space, and his acceleration over the first two or three yards is so good he leaves most defenders standing. When he gets into the area, one of his great strengths is that he can snatch at a shot and still get some power into it. He hardly needs any back-lift."

Joachim's skills have also seen him recognised at international where he has represented England at Youth and Under-21 level.

When he was transferred to Aston Villa for £1.5m in February 1996, a full England cap beckoned. But, with the likes of Dwight Yorke and Stan Collymore ahead of him, he was unable to maintain a consistent first team place. Midway through the 1997/98 season there was talk that his patience had run out and he was prepared to leave in order to get regular first team football.

After a spell in the wilderness, Joachim got a sustained run in the Villa side in February 1998 and recommenced first team duties following Yorke's departure to Manchester United in September 1998.

Julian Joachim is an ambitious player and one day sees himself playing on foreign fields. He was quoted in a magazine as saying: "I would like to play in Europe at some stage in my career. I know that sounds ambitious but that's what I would like to do. I just want to go as far in the game as I possibly can."

Leonard Johnrose

BURY

Midfielder

Nationality:	English
Place of Birth:	Preston
Date of Birth:	29 November 1969
Height:	5'1"
Club History:	Blackburn Rovers Preston North End Hartlepool United

David Johnson

IPSWICH TOWN

Forward

Nationality:	English/Jamaican
Place of Birth:	Jamaica
Date of Birth:	15 August 1976
Height:	5'6"
Club History:	Manchester United Bury
Honours/Caps:	Second Division Championship 1997 with Bury

David Johnson used to share the same dressing room with the likes of Manchester United's Paul Scholes and Nicky Butt during his early career. In 1995, Johnson left the 'Theatre of Dreams' and headed for Gigg Lane, the home of Bury. Johnson carved a name for himself by helping Bury to climb up the Divisions, and in 1997 he moved to Ipswich.

Along with his domestic commitments, Johnson has attracted the attention of no fewer than three international sides - Northern Ireland, England and Jamaica - where he qualifies to play for all three!

David Johnson

Marvin Johnson

LUTON TOWN

Forward

Nationality: English
Place of Birth: Middlesex
Date of Birth: 29 October 1968
Height: 5′11″

Michael Johnson

BIRMINGHAM CITY

Defender

Nationality: English
Place of Birth: Nottingham
Date of Birth: 4 July 1973
Height: 5′11′

Keith Jones

CHARLTON ATHLETIC

Midfielder

Nationality: English
Place of Birth: London
Date of Birth: 14 October 1965
Height: 5′9″
Club History: Chelsea
Brentford
Southend United

Marc Joseph

CAMBRIDGE UNITED

Defender

Nationality: English
Place of Birth: Leicester
Date of Birth: 10 November 1976
Height: 6′1″

Matthew Joseph

CAMBRIDGE UNITED

Defender

Nationality: English
Place of Birth: London
Date of Birth: 30 September 1972
Height: 5′7″
Club History: Arsenal
Gillingham

Roger Joseph

LEYTON ORIENT

Defender

Nationality: English
Place of Birth: London
Date of Birth: 24 December 1965
Height: 5′11″
Club History: Brentford
Wimbledon
Millwall
West Bromwich Albion
Honours/Caps: Cap for England B

Mark Jules

CHESTERFIELD

Forward

Nationality: English
Place of Birth: Bradford
Date of Birth: 5 September 1971
Height: 5′1″
Club History: Bradford City
Scarborough

Nwankwo Kanu

ARSENAL

Forward

Nationality: Nigerian
Place of Birth: Nigeria
Height: 6′0″
Honours/Caps: European Cup 1995 with Ajax

Nwankwo Kanu

John Keister

WALSALL

Midfielder

Nationality: English
Place of Birth: Walsall
Date of Birth: 11 November 1970
Height: 5'8"

Darren Kenton

NORWICH CITY

Midfielder

Nationality: English
Place of Birth: London
Date of Birth: 13 September 1978
Height: 5'9"

Andy Kiwomya

BRADFORD CITY

Forward

Nationality: English
Place of Birth: Huddersfield
Date of Birth: 1 October 1967
Height: 5'9"
Club History: Barnsley
Sheffield Wednesday
Dundee United
Rotherham United
Halifax Town
Scunthorpe United
Luton Town

Chris Kiwomya

QUEENS PARK RANGERS

Forward

Nationality: English
Place of Birth: Huddersfield
Date of Birth: 2 December 1969
Height: 5'9"
Club History: Ipswich Town
Arsenal
Huddersfield Town
Honours/Caps: Second Division Championship
1992 with Ipswich Town

Nyamah Kofi

STOKE CITY

Midfielder

Nationality: English
Place of Birth: London
Date of Birth: 20 June 1975
Height: 5'1"
Club History: Cambridge United
Kettering

Michael Kyd

CAMBRIDGE UNITED

Forward

Nationality: English
Place of Birth: London
Date of Birth: 21 May 1977
Height: 5'11"

Bernard Lambourde

CHELSEA

Defender

Nationality: French
Place of Birth: Guadeloupe
Date of Birth: 11 May 1971
Height: 6'2"
Club History: Bordeaux

James Lawrence

BRADFORD CITY

Forward

Nationality: English
Place of Birth: London
Date of Birth: 8 March 1970
Height: 5'1"
Club History: Cowes
Sunderland
Doncaster Rovers
Leicester City

Des Lyttle

Carl Leaburn

WIMBLEDON

Forward

Nationality: English
Place of Birth: London
Date of Birth: 30 March 1969
Height: 6'3"
Club History: Northampton Town
Honours/Caps: Caps for England Youth and England Under 19s

Jason Lee

WATFORD

Forward

Nationality: English
Place of Birth: London
Date of Birth: 9 May 1971
Height: 6'3"
Club History: Charlton Athletic
Stockport County
Lincoln City
Southend United
Nottingham Forest
Grimsby Town

Neil Lewis

PETERBOROUGH UNITED

Forward

Nationality: English
Place of Birth: Wolverhampton
Date of Birth: 28 June 1974
Height: 5'7"
Club History: Leicester City

Des Linton

PETERBOROUGH UNITED

Defender

Nationality: English
Place of Birth: Birmingham
Date of Birth: 5 September 1971
Height: 6'1"
Club History: Leicester City
Luton Town

Kevin Lisbie

CHARLTON ATHLETIC

Forward

Nationality: English
Place of Birth: London
Date of Birth: 17 October 1978
Height: 5'10"

Adrian Littlejohn

BURY

Midfielder

Nationality: English
Place of Birth: Wolverhampton
Date of Birth: 26 September 1970
Height: 5'9"
Club History: Wolverhampton Wanderers
West Bromwich Albion
Wallsall
Sheffield United

Des Lyttle

NOTTINGHAM FOREST

Defender

Nationality: English
Place of Birth: Wolverhampton
Date of Birth: 24 September 1971
Height: 5'9"
Club History: Leicester City
Worcester City
Swansea City

Danny Maddix

Danny Maddix

QUEENS PARK RANGERS

Defender

Nationality:	English
Place of Birth:	Kent
Date of Birth:	11 October 1967
Height:	5'1"
Club History:	Tottenham Hotspur
	Southend United
Honours/Caps:	Caps for Jamaica

Danny Maddix has been a stalwart for the west London side since he joined them on a free transfer from Tottenham in 1987. In between his employment with the two London clubs, Maddix had a two-match loan spell with Southend United.

Still a good friend of former Ranger, Les Ferdinand, Maddix has had something of a yo-yo existence in the Rangers side. Several changes of manager have not helped this competent defender (or man marker).

Maddix made his debut for Jamaica in April 1998, but failed to make their 1998 World Cup squad.

Michael Mahoney-Johnson

QUEENS PARK RANGERS

Forward

Nationality:	English
Place of Birth:	London
Date of Birth:	6 November 1976
Height:	5'1"
Club History:	Wycombe Wanderers

Paul Mahorn

TOTTENHAM HOTSPUR

Forward

Nationality:	English
Place of Birth:	London
Date of Birth:	13 August 1973
Height:	5'10"
Club History:	Fulham
	Burnley
	Brentford

Clint Marcelle

BARNSLEY

Forward

Nationality:	Trinidadian
Place of Birth:	Port of Spain, Trinidad
Date of Birth:	9 November 1968
Height:	5'4"
Club History:	Falgueiras, Trinidad
Honours/Caps:	Caps for Trinidad and Tobago

Clint Marcelle joined Barnsley in August 1996. Since then the progress of both parties has been meteoric. As defenders in the Premiership and First Division have found out, the diminutive Marcelle is one of the game's quickest forwards. Barnsley's promotion to the Premiership in the 1996/97 season was largely due to a cultured, attacking style of play. Marcelle, with his eight goals, was an integral part of that successful team.

Dwight Marshall

LUTON TOWN

Forward

Nationality:	Jamaican/English
Place of Birth:	Jamaica
Date of Birth:	3 October 1965
Height:	5'11"
Club History:	Grays Athletic
	Plymouth Argyle
	Middlesbrough

Ken Monkou

Jae Martin

LINCOLN CITY

Forward

Nationality:	English
Place of Birth:	London
Date of Birth:	5 February 1976
Height:	5'11"
Club History:	Southend United Leyton Orient Birmingham City

Ronald Mauge

PLYMOUTH ARGYLE

Midfielder

Nationality:	English
Place of Birth:	London
Date of Birth:	10 March 1969
Height:	5'1"
Club History:	Charlton Athletic Fulham Bury

Rodney McDonald

CHESTER CITY

Forward

Nationality:	English
Place of Birth:	London
Date of Birth:	20 March 1967
Height:	5'10"
Club History:	Walsall Partick Thistle

Andy McFarlane

TORQUAY UNITED

Midfielder

Nationality:	English
Place of Birth:	Wolverhampton
Date of Birth:	30 November 1968
Height:	6'3"
Club History:	Cradley Heath Portsmouth Swansea City Scunthorpe United

Gavin McGowan

ARSENAL

Midfielder

Nationality:	English
Place of Birth:	London
Date of Birth:	16 January 1976
Height:	5'11'
Club History:	Luton Town
Honours/Caps:	Caps for England Youth

Keith McPherson

READING

Defender

Nationality:	English
Place of Birth:	London
Date of Birth:	11 September 1963
Height:	5'11"
Club History:	West Ham United Cambridge United Northampton Town

Ken Monkou

SOUTHAMPTON

Defender

Nationality:	Dutch
Place of Birth:	Surinam
Date of Birth:	29 November 1964
Height:	6'0"
Club History:	Feyenoord Chelsea
Honours/Caps:	One Cap for Holland Under 21s

One of the major reasons why Southampton have held on to their Premiership status over the years is due, in part, to the defensive stability and athleticism of Ken Monkou. Relegation battles are a regular feature, but each year they manage a last-minute lifeline.
His battles to keep the south coast club up with the big boys, is light years away from where Monkou started his career.
His first professional signing was for Dutch giants, Feyenoord, and in 1989 he got his break in England with Chelsea in a deal worth

£100,000. After 94 league appearances for the Blues, and just days into the 1992/93 season, he made a shock transfer to Southampton for £750,000.

Darren Moore

BRADFORD CITY

Defender

Nationality: English
Place of Birth: Birmingham
Date of Birth: 22 April 1974
Height: 6'2"
Club History: Torquay United
Doncaster Rovers

Jao Moreira

SWANSEA CITY

Defender

Nationality: Portuguese
Place of Birth: Oporto, Portugal
Date of Birth: 30 June 1970
Height: 6'3"
Club History: Benfica

Stephen Morgan

WIGAN ATHLETIC

Defender

Nationality: English
Place of Birth: Oldham
Date of Birth: 19 September 1968
Height: 6'0"
Club History: Blackpool
Plymouth Argyle
Coventry City
Bristol Rovers

Andrew Morris

CHESTERFIELD

Forward

Nationality: English
Place of Birth: Sheffield
Date of Birth: 17 November 1967
Height: 6'4"
Club History: Rotherham United
Exeter City

Paul Mortimer

CHARTLON ATHLETIC

Midfielder/Forward

Nationality: English
Place of Birth: London
Date of Birth: 8 May 1968
Height: 5'11"
Club History: Aston Villa
Crystal Palace
Brentford
Honours/Caps: England Under 21

Injuries have blighted the career of the left-sided midfielder/attacker. While Charlton regained their top flight status - and attempted to preserve it - Paul Mortimer was often to be found on the treatment table trying to recover from another untimely setback. When he has been available for selection he has scored important goals or contributed with a deft pass. His experience and know-how may well prove beneficial to Charlton, no matter what division they are in.

Andy Myers

CHELSEA

Defender

Nationality: English
Place of Birth: Middlesex
Date of Birth: 3 November 1973
Height: 5'8"
Honours/Caps: FA Cup 1997 with Chelsea
League Cup 1998 with Chelsea
European Cup Winners' Cup 1998 with Chelsea
Four Caps for England Under 21s

Like many of Chelsea's home-grown talent, Andy Myers is facing something of a dilemma. Should he stay with the club and battle for a regular first team place, or will the power of Gianluca Vialli's cheque book, and the acquisition of new players, force him to finally leave his only professional club?

If his gritty performances on the field are anything to go by, Myers will probably stay and fight for his place. That would be understandable as he has already tasted success at the club when his team beat Middlesbrough in 1997 to win the FA Cup.

Myers was often seen on the bench kicking his heels while a former Blues' boss, Ruud Gullitt's foreign legion took the west London club to heights they had not reached for decades.

Player/manager Luca Vialli likes players with credentials and Myers possesses some of his own. He has already represented England at Under-21, Youth and Schoolboy level. Being a part of the Vialli revival can only make Myers a better player.

George Ndah

SWINDON TOWN

Forward

Nationality: English
Place of Birth: London
Date of Birth: 23 December 1974
Height: 6'1"
Club History: Crystal Palace
Bournemouth

Peter Ndlovu

BIRMINGHAM CITY

Forward

Nationality: Zimbabwean
Place of Birth: Zimbabwe
Date of Birth: 25 February 1973
Height: 5'8"
Club History: Highlanders
Coventry City
Honours/Caps: Caps for Zimbabwe

Peter Ndlovu's failure to carve out a bigger name for himself continues to puzzle almost everyone who has seen him play. The diminutive Ndlovu is the Zimbabwe international who shot to prominence in England in 1991 with his fleet-footed displays with Coventry City. After a £20,000 move from Zimbabwe club side, Highlanders, Ndlovu's career appeared to have no limits as spectators marvelled at his repertoire of sleight-of-foot tricks and goals.

He scored 41 times during 197 times for Coventry before his departure to Birmingham City in July 1997.

Eddie Newton

CHELSEA

Midfielder

Nationality: English
Place of Birth: London
Date of Birth: 13 December 1971
Height: 6'0"
Club History: Cardiff City
Honours/Caps: FA Cup 1997 with Chelsea
League Cup 1998 with Chelsea
European Cup Winners' Cup 1998 with Chelsea
Two Caps for England Under 21s

In the words of Mark Hughes - a man with a second-to-none record of four FA Cup winners' medals - scoring a goal in a Final is the greatest experience a player can have in the domestic game.

Well, 'steady' Eddie Newton has had that experience. It was the lithe, hard tackling

Peter Ndlovu

Eddie Newton

Shaun Newton

Newton who scored Chelsea's second, and clinching goal against Middlesbrough in the 82nd minute of the 1997 Final at Wembley. That goal was the only time that Newton got his name on the score-sheet all season.
It was the first piece of silverware that Newton and his club had collected for over two decades. Under the shrewd guidance of living legends, Ruud Gullitt and then Luca Vialli, Chelsea seem destined to add to that wonderful day in May 1997. But what part will Newton play?
He has been dogged by many injuries and, consequently, has been pushed down the pecking order. In the 1996/97 season he started a mere 13 games and was twice a substitute.

Shaun Newton

CHARLTON ATHLETIC

Midfielder

Nationality: English
Place of Birth: London
Date of Birth: 20 August 1975
Height: 5'8"

Shaun Newton is a busy, hard tackling midfielder. His form played an integral part in Charlton's promotion to the Premiership during the 1997/98 season.

Gifton Noel-Williams

WATFORD

Forward

Nationality: English
Place of Birth: London
Date of Birth: 21 January 1980
Height: 6'1"

Charles Ntamark

WALSALL

Midfielder

Nationality: English
Place of Birth: London
Date of Birth: 22 July 1970
Height: 5'8"
Club History: Borehamwood

Emeka Nwadike

SHREWSBURY TOWN

Defender

Nationality: English
Place of Birth: London
Date of Birth: 9 August 1978
Height: 6'0"
Club History: Wolverhampton Wanderers

Martin O'Connor

BIRMINGHAM CITY

Midfielder

Nationality: English
Place of Birth: Walsall
Date of Birth: 10 December 1967
Height: 5'8"
Club History: Bromsgrove Rovers
Crystal Palace
Walsall
Peterborough United

John O'Kane

EVERTON

Defender

Nationality: English
Place of Birth: Nottingham
Date of Birth: 15 November 1974
Height: 5'10"
Club History: Manchester United
Wimbledon
Bury

Carlton Palmer

Joseph Omigie

BRENTFORD

Forward

Nationality: English
Place of Birth: London
Date of Birth: 13 June 1972
Height: 6'2"
Club History: Donna
Woking

Emmanuel Omoyinmi

WEST HAM UNITED

Forward

Nationality: Nigerian
Place of Birth: Nigeria
Date of Birth: 28 December 1977
Height: 5'6"
Club History: Bournemouth
Dundee United

Ifem Onoura

SWINDON TOWN

Midfielder

Nationality: Scottish
Place of Birth: Glasgow
Date of Birth: 28 July 1967
Height: 6'0"
Club History: Huddersfield Town
Mansfield Town

Udo Onwere

BARNET

Midfielder

Nationality: English
Place of Birth: London
Date of Birth: 9 November 1971
Height: 6'0"
Club History: Fulham
Lincoln City
Dover Athletic
Blackpool

Ricky Otto

BIRMINGHAM CITY

Forward

Nationality: English
Place of Birth: London
Date of Birth: 9 November 1967
Height: 5'9"
Club History: Leyton Orient
Southend United
Charlton Athletic
Peterborough United
Honours/Caps: Second Division Championship 1995 with Birmingham City

Careers do not get more nomadic than the one experienced by Ricky Otto. The East Ender began his professional career at his local club, Leyton Orient, and has since gone on to play for another five clubs with varying degrees of success. Otto, noted for his dribbling skills, joined City in December 1994 having left Southend United for the Midlands club for £800,000. Since his move to Birmingham he has been on loan twice to Charlton Athletic and Peterborough United.

Carlton Palmer

NOTTINGHAM FOREST

Midfielder

Nationality: English
Place of Birth: West Midlands
Date of Birth: 5 December 1965
Height: 6'2"
Club History: West Bromwich Albion
Sheffield Wednesday
Leeds United
Southampton
Honours/Caps: 18 Caps for England

Not too many players earn 18 England caps and come in for such ridicule as Carlton Palmer. It may have had something to do with the fact that Palmer earned the bulk of his international recognition during the reign of the equally maligned Graham Taylor.
Palmer's lack of media popularity stems from his sometimes ungainly action - something of a

windmill impression - and the fact that he could care less what the media thinks.

One man who thinks the world of the six-footer is Ron Atkinson, who gave Palmer his break at West Bromwich Albion, took him to Sheffield Wednesday and now Nottingham Forest. Indeed, when Atkinson was to briefly manage Wednesday again late in 1997, he tried to make Palmer his first acquisition, but the big man left Leeds United for Southampton.

Palmer may not be a goal-scorer - less than 30 goals in more than 450 games - but he is a spoiler, whose sole intention is to break up the opposition's approach play. And this he does with devastating effect.

Dennis Pearce

NOTTS COUNTY

Defender

Nationality:	English
Place of Birth:	Wolverhampton
Date of Birth:	10 September 1974
Height:	5'9"
Club History:	Aston Villa
	Wolverhampton Wanderers

Martin Pemberton

DONCASTER ROVERS

Midfielder

Nationality:	English
Place of Birth:	Bradford
Date of Birth:	1 February 1976
Height:	5'8"
Club History:	Oldham Athletic

Robert Petta

IPSWICH TOWN

Forward

Nationality:	Dutch
Place of Birth:	Rotterdam
Date of Birth:	6 August 1974
Height:	5'7"

Terry Phelan

EVERTON

Defender

Nationality:	Irish
Place of Birth:	Manchester
Date of Birth:	16 February 1967
Height:	5'8"
Club History:	Leeds United
	Swansea City
	Wimbledon
	Manchester City
	Chelsea
Honours/Caps:	FA Cup 1988 with Wimbledon
	37 Caps for Republic of Ireland

Republic of Ireland left-back Terry Phelan made his name as part of the Wimbledon 'Crazy Gang' that defied all the odds to defeat mighty Liverpool in the 1988 FA Cup Final.

The nimble defender will forever be a hero in south-west London due to that heady May day over a decade ago. Phelan has plied his trade at clubs up and down the country. The Phelan story started in the north with Leeds United in 1984. Having played just 19 times for the Yorkshire giants he was given a free transfer to Swansea City two years later.

He was to join Wimbledon for a modest £100,000 just a year before their greatest day at Wembley against all-conquering Liverpool. He played over 200 League and Cup games for the game's biggest party-poopers before he headed north once again, this time to join Manchester City for £2.5m in 1992.

Since his departure from Maine Road he has been involved in two near £1m transfers. Chelsea were next to invest in his talents for £900,000 and two years later, in January 1997, Everton were to become his third northern employers after a £850,000 move.

One can see that Phelan's career, and his transfer value, has continually improved over the years. His Everton career has been on something of a pause after injury and several changes in management. At the start of the World Cup year, a first-team place at Goodison was far from guaranteed.

Away from the domestic game, Phelan has

represented his country nearly forty times. Phelan, quite often to be seen marauding into the opposition penalty area, was part of Jack Charlton and the Republic's love affair with the World Cup during the Nineties. This little nation's success in the world's leading tournament was due, in part, to the skill and application of the likes of Phelan.

Dwayne Plummer

BRISTOL CITY

Defender

Nationality: English
Place of Birth: Bristol
Date of Birth: 12 December 1976
Height: 6'3"

Stephane Pounewatchy

CARLISLE UNITED

Defender

Nationality: French
Place of Birth: Paris
Date of Birth: 10 February 1968
Height: 6'0"
Club History: Gueugnon

Chris Powell

CHARLTON ATHLETIC

Defender

Nationality: English
Place of Birth: London
Date of Birth: 8 September 1969
Height: 5'1"
Club History: Crystal Palace
Aldershot
Southend United
Derby County

Chris Powell is a quick, mobile defender. Having joined Derby from Southend for £750,000 in June 1995, he is one of the most improved players in the Premiership. His form was one of the vital factors in Derby's improved position during the 1997/98 season.

Powell served most of his League football apprenticeship at Southend United and made over 200 appearances for the seaside club, proving to be a golden nugget in a very ordinary team.

If he can earn a call from Jamaica, Chris Powell's career at club and international level would appear to be soaring.

Powell was transferred to Premiership newcomers Charlton Athletic just prior to the 1998/99 season.

Darryl Powell

DERBY COUNTY

Midfielder

Nationality: English
Place of Birth: London
Date of Birth: 15 November 1971
Height: 6'0"
Club History: Portsmouth
Honours/Caps: Five Caps for Jamaica

Andrew Preece

BLACKPOOL

Forward

Nationality: English
Place of Birth: Evesham
Date of Birth: 27 March 1967
Height: 6'1"
Club History: Evesham
Northampton Town
Worcester City
Wrexham
Stockport County
Crystal Palace

Chris Powell

Jason Price

SWANSEA CITY

Midfielder

Nationality: Welsh
Place of Birth: Aberdare, Wales
Date of Birth: 12 April 1977
Height: 6'2"
Club History: Aberaman Athletic

Nigel Quashie

NOTTINGHAM FOREST

Midfielder

Nationality: English
Place of Birth: London
Date of Birth: 20 July 1978
Height: 5'9"
Club History: Queens Park Rangers
Honours/Caps: Caps for England B

As England's B team surprisingly lost 2-0 to Chile in February 1998, one observer suggested that young Nigel Quashie reminded him of Paul Ince. The comparison was valid. Quashie was to be seen that night at West Bromwich Albion's Hawthorns ground, firstly breaking up Chile's attacks before participating in forays intending to penetrate the South Americans' goal. The youngster has a marvellous engine and physical presence.
Just one week into the 1998/99 season, Quashie was sold to Nottingham Forest for £2.5m.

Lucas Radebe

LEEDS UNITED

Defender

Nationality: South African
Place of Birth: Johannesburg
Date of Birth: 12 April 1969
Height: 6'0"
Club History: Kaizer Chiefs
Honours/Caps: 44 Caps for South Africa

Lucas Radebe's rise to prominence has been dream stuff. Plucked from obscurity by former Leeds supremo Howard Wilkinson in September 1994, this hard-tackling defender has proved to be an essential cog for both club and country.
Formerly with South Africa's leading club, Kaiser Chiefs, Radebe is the captain of the South African team who entered the 1998 World Cup in France determined to continue the positive emergence of African nations on the international stage.
For Leeds he has proved to be the rock that boss David O'Leary has built his team on. Essentially, Radebe is a central defender, but O'Leary has occasionally used him to man mark the opposition's most influential player. Radebe possesses tenacity, durability and also has the ability to distribute the ball effectively, unlike so many defenders in the English game.
When Leeds spent £2.6m on the Johannesburg-born Radebe they cannot have imagined that it would have been one of their better foreign investments.
Radebe ended up the losing captain as favourites South Africa were beaten 2-0 by Egypt in the final of the African Nations Cup at the end of February 1998.

Isaiah Rankin

BRADFORD CITY

Forward

Nationality: English
Place of Birth: London
Date of Birth: 22 May 1978
Height: 5'10"
Club History: Arsenal
Honours/Caps: Caps for England Youth

Mark Rankine

PRESTON NORTH END

Midfielder

Nationality: English
Place of Birth: Doncaster
Date of Birth: 30 September 1969
Height: 5'1"
Club History: Doncaster Rovers
Wolverhampton Wanderers

Lucas Radebe

Kevin Rattray

BARNET

Midfielder

Nationality: English
Place of Birth: London
Date of Birth: 6 October 1968
Height: 5'11"
Club History: Woking
Gillingham

Dean Richards

WOLVERHAMPTON WANDERERS

Defender

Nationality: English
Place of Birth: Bradford
Date of Birth: 9 June 1974
Height: 6'0"
Club History: Bradford City
Honours/Caps: Four Caps for England Under 21s

Still only in his mid-twenties, we have not yet seen the best of the highly-rated Dean Richards. The powerful central defender began his career with home town club, Bradford City. He was to play just 67 games for the club before Wolves made him their record transfer, at £1.3m, in 1995. Since then injury - the scourge of Richards in particular and Wolves in general - has denied him his expected progress. The grapevine suggests that if he can stay clear of injury, Richards may well replace one of the four ageing stars in Arsenal's defence.

Hamilton Ricard

MIDDLESBROUGH

Foward

Nationality: Colombian
Place of Birth: Colombia
Date of Birth: 12 January 1974
Height: 6'2"
Club History: Deportivo Cali

All credit must be given to the Colombian international, Hamilton Ricard. His early days with Boro were the proverbial "horror story" for a player who has yet to get a firm grasp of the English language.

However, football's most important language is goals. Hamilton Ricard, after looking like he would fail to hit a barn door, is enjoying his goal-scoring best spell in the English Premiership.

Midway through the 1998/99 season, Ricard was hitting the target enough to ensure that Middlesbrough were among the top half-dozen in the league.

His pace, strength and ability to shoot with either foot saw him slowly overcome the criticisms that had been directed toward him in his early days in the north-east.

Michael Ricketts

WALSALL

Forward

Nationality: English
Place of Birth: Birmingham
Date of Birth: 4 December 1978
Height: 5'8"

Neville Roach

READING

Forward

Nationality: English
Place of Birth: Reading
Date of Birth: 29 September 1978
Height: 5'10"

Jason Rockett

SCARBOROUGH

Midfielder

Nationality: English
Place of Birth: London
Date of Birth: 26 September 1969
Height: 5'11"
Club History: Rotherham United

Michael Rodosthenous

WEST BROMWICH ALBION

Midfielder

Nationality: English
Place of Birth: London
Date of Birth: 25 August 1976
Height: 5'11"

Leo Roget

SOUTHEND UNITED

Defender

Nationality: English
Place of Birth: Essex
Date of Birth: 1 August 1977
Height: 6'1"
Club History: Dover Athletic

Rodney Rowe

YORK CITY

Forward

Nationality: English
Place of Birth: Huddersfield
Date of Birth: 30 July 1975
Height: 5'8"
Club History: Huddersfield Town
Scarborough
Bury

Zeke Rowe

PETERBOROUGH UNITED

Midfielder

Nationality: English
Place of Birth: London
Date of Birth: 30 October 1973
Height: 5'10"
Club History: Chelsea
Barnet

Richard Rufus

CHARLTON ATHLETIC

Defender

Nationality: English
Place of Birth: London
Date of Birth: 12 January 1975
Height: 6'1"
Honours/Caps: Six Caps for England Under 21s

Matthew Rush

OLDHAM ATHLETIC

Midfielder

Nationality: English
Place of Birth: London
Date of Birth: 6 August 1971
Height: 5'11"
Club History: West Ham United
Cambridge United
Swansea City
Norwich City
Northampton Town

John Salako

FULHAM

Forward

Nationality: English
Place of Birth: Nigeria
Date of Birth: 11 February 1959
Height: 5'9"
Club History: Crystal Palace
Swansea
Bolton Wanderers
Coventry City
Honours/Caps: First Division Championship 1994 with Crystal Palace
Five Caps for England

Few remember that it was fleet-footed John Salako who set-up many of the goal-scoring chances for the Crystal Palace strike duo of Ian Wright and Mark Bright. He made 200 appearances for Palace and helped them to the First Division Championship in 1994. He also attracted the attention of England bosses and gained five caps for his country.

Richard Rufus

John Salako celebrates with team-mate Dirk Lehmann

His form was not to be repeated at Coventry, where long-term injury restricted his ability and opportunities.
In January 1998, Coventry boss Gordon Strachan put him on the transfer list after he rejected the offer of a new contract. It was anticipated that Salako would take advantage of the Bosman ruling, which allows players to free-transfer within Europe, and Dutch giants Feyenoord expressed more than a passing interest in acquiring his services.
But it was Premiership strugglers Bolton Wanderers who captured the winger's services in a loan deal just moments before the transfer deadline in March 1998. However, and only months later,
John Salako returned to London as part of Kevin Keegan's Fulham.

Dean Samuels

BARNET

Forward

Nationality:	English
Place of Birth:	London
Date of Birth:	29 March 1973
Height:	6'2"
Club History:	Borehamwood

Richard Shaw

COVENTRY CITY

Defender

Nationality:	English
Place of Birth:	London
Date of Birth:	11 September 1968
Height:	5'9"
Club History:	Crystal Palace Hull City
Honours/Caps:	First Division Championship 1994 with Crystal Palace

In the early Nineties, Crystal Palace were a vibrant and competitive outfit who gave the so-called more fashionable teams more than a run for their money. And the quiet one at the back, marshalling their defence, was Richard Shaw.

Now plying his trade in the Midlands with ambitious Coventry City, he was one of several big names who quit Crystal Palace when they lost their Premiership status in 1995.
But before that he had been a loyal servant to the south London outfit where he played over 200 league games for the club and contributed to their successful FA Cup run in 1995.
His versatility makes him a more than useful asset to his employers. He can play at either full-back or centre-half, and it is this flexibility that will ensure he is one of the first choices for City boss, Gordon Strachan.

Fitzroy Simpson

PORTSMOUTH

Midfielder

Nationality:	Jamaican
Place of Birth:	Wiltshire
Date of Birth:	26 February 1970
Height:	5'6"
Club History:	Swindon Town Manchester City
Honours/Caps:	21 Caps for Jamaica

While Portsmouth languish at the bottom of the First Division, Fitzroy Simpson's international career continues to surge forward. A dynamic, hard-working midfielder, Simpson was one of the British-based players that beefed up Jamaica's World Cup bid in France 98. Apart from his hard work in Jamaica's engine-room, he is capable of scoring a goal or two.
He transferred from his home town club, Swindon Town, to Manchester City for £500,000 in March 1992. The move to City did not fulfil his potential and three years later he moved to Portsmouth.

Frank Sinclair stands firm against Kevin Davies

Philip Simpson

BARNET

Midfielder

Nationality:	English
Place of Birth:	London
Date of Birth:	19 October 1969
Height:	5'8"
Club History:	Stevenage Borough

Frank Sinclair

LEICESTER CITY

Defender

Nationality:	English
Place of Birth:	London
Date of Birth:	3 December 1971
Height:	5'9"
Club History:	West Bromwich Albion
	Chelsea
Honours/Caps:	FA Cup 1997 with Chelsea
	League Cup 1998 with Chelsea
	13 Caps for Jamaica

Frank Sinclair was one of the first major casualties of Chelsea's cosmopolitan approach to winning the Premiership. In August 1998, he was considered surplus to requirements and sold to Leicester City for £2m.

One of the highlights of his career came when he was selected to play for Jamaica against Brazil during the World Cup in February 1998.

Trevor Sinclair

WEST HAM UNITED

Midfielder

Nationality:	English
Place of Birth:	London
Date of Birth:	2 March 1973
Height:	5'1"
Club History:	Blackpool
	Queens Park Rangers
Honours/Caps:	21 Caps for England Under 21s

Trevor Sinclair made his mark, and proved his worth, within days of signing for West Ham United on 31 January 1998. His debut performance could not have been better.

Having signed his contract - worth £3m - on the Thursday, Sinclair was to pay back some of his hefty fee with two goals for the Hammers in their 2-2 draw against Everton two days later.

Like Manchester United's Andy Cole, Trevor Sinclair is a product of the Football Association's School of Excellence - the brainchild of former national boss Bobby Robson and Charles Hughes. The school is the springboard for many young footballers who have been earmarked for future England teams because of their skill and potential.

Before he left Queens Park Rangers - where he made 160 appearances - Sinclair had won 21 England Under-21 caps. His electric skills, and equally exciting goals, marked him as a full international of the future. But with Rangers' decline and their internal wranglings, Sinclair seemed to lose his way. The move to West Ham has changed all that.

West Ham boss, Harry Redknapp commented on Sinclair's career to date: "Just 18 months ago he was rated at £7m, setting the world on fire and forcing his way into the England squad. He is talented and versatile and can play wide, as a forward or even off the front man."

Steve Slade

QUEENS PARK RANGERS

Forward

Nationality:	English
Place of Birth:	Essex
Date of Birth:	6 October 1975
Height:	5'11'
Club History:	Tottenham Hotspur
	Brentford

Trevor Sinclair

Jamie Smith

CRYSTAL PALACE

Defender

Nationality: English
Place of Birth: Birmingham
Date of Birth: 17 September 1974
Height: 5'6"
Club History: Wolverhampton Wanderers

Peter Smith

BRIGHTON & HOVE ALBION

Defender

Nationality: English
Place of Birth: Stone
Date of Birth: 12 July 1969
Height: 6'1"
Club History: Alma Swanley

Rigobert Song

LIVERPOOL

Defender

Nationality: Cameroonian
Place of Birth: Cameroon
Height: 6'2"
Club History: Salernitana

The Cameroon international defender holds a distinction which will not be the envy of his peers.
Rigobert Song will go down in the history books as the first man to be sent off in two successive World Cup Finals tournaments. His indiscretions on the pitch saw him take an early bath in 1994 and 1998.
Even so, Liverpool were so convinced of his talents they signed him for £2.6m from Serie A club, Salernitana.

Mark Stein

BOURNEMOUTH

Forward

Nationality: English
Place of Birth: South Africa
Date of Birth: 28 January 1966
Height: 5'6"
Club History: Luton Town
Aldershot
Queen's Park Rangers
Oxford United
Stoke City
Ipswich Town
Bournemouth
Chelsea
Honours/Caps: League Cup 1988 with Luton Town
Second Division Championship 1993 with Stoke City
Three Caps for England Under 19s

Worrell Sterling

LINCOLN CITY

Midfielder

Nationality: English
Place of Birth: London
Date of Birth: 8 June 1965
Height: 5'7"
Club History: Watford
Peterborough United
Bristol Rovers

Dean Stokes

PORT VALE

Defender

Nationality: English
Place of Birth: Birmingham
Date of Birth: 23 May 1970
Height: 5'7"
Club History: Halesowen Town

Rigobert Song engages with John Barnes

Dean Sturridge scores for Derby

Dean Sturridge

DERBY COUNTY

Forward

Nationality: English
Place of Birth: Birmingham
Date of Birth: 27 July 1973
Height: 5'8"
Club History: Torquay United

Dean Sturridge has played his part in the Derby revival and is seen as something of a hero by the fans. Before the 1997/98 season, he scored an impressive 32 goals in 90 appearances for the club. Even when on loan to Torquay United, he found the back of the net five times in just ten games.

Simon Sturridge

STOKE CITY

Forward

Nationality: English
Place of Birth: Birmingham
Date of Birth: 9 December 1969
Height: 5'5"
Club History: Birmingham City

Ian Taylor

ASTON VILLA

Midfielder

Nationality: English
Place of Birth: Birmingham
Date of Birth: 4 June 1968
Height: 6'1"
Club History: Moor Green
Port Vale
Sheffield Wednesday
Honours/Caps: League Cup 1996 with Aston Villa

Ian Taylor is the type of dependable player that all managers need. No fuss, no histrionics, just an innate ability to churn out steady, workman-like performances week in week out.
Born in the Midlands, Taylor's professional career started in the football backwaters of Port Vale. In July 1992, Vale snapped up the midfielder's talents for a meagre £15,000 having seen him make an impression with his first club, Moor Green.
Since then, Taylor, a ball-winning, box-to-box player, has been involved in two £1m moves. His first taste of the big time came with Sheffield Wednesday exactly two years after his move to Port Vale.
Just five months later he was to receive a surprise present as Aston Villa were to secure his services just four days before Christmas 1994. It was with Villa that he was to put his hands on his only honour to date.
Taylor was one of the goal-scorers in the Villa team that thrashed Leeds United 3-0 in the Final of the Coca-Cola Cup in 1996. His contribution, of late, has been instrumental in Villa's rise to prominence in 1998/99.

Lee Taylor

SHREWSBURY TOWN

Defender

Nationality: English
Place of Birth: London
Date of Birth: 24 February 1976
Height: 5'11"

Mark Taylor

SHREWSBURY TOWN

Forward

Nationality: English
Place of Birth: Birmingham
Date of Birth: 22 February 1966
Height: 5'8"
Club History: Walsall
Sheffield Wednesday

Ian Taylor

Mitchell Thomas

LUTON TOWN

Defender

Nationality: English
Place of Birth: Luton
Date of Birth: 2 October 1964
Height: 6'0"
Club History: Tottenham Hotspur
West Ham United

Roderick Thomas

CHESTER CITY

Forward

Nationality: English
Place of Birth: London
Date of Birth: 10 October 1970
Height: 5'6"
Club History: Watford
Gillingham
Carlisle United

Wayne Thomas

TORQUAY UNITED

Midfielder

Nationality: English
Place of Birth: Walsall
Date of Birth: 28 August 1978
Height: 5'11"

Gary Thompson

NORTHAMPTON TOWN

Forward

Nationality: English
Place of Birth: Birmingham
Date of Birth: 7 October 1959
Height: 6'1"
Club History: West Bromwich Albion
Sheffield Wednesday
Aston Villa
Watford
Crystal Palace
Queens Park Rangers
Cardiff City

Jeffrey Thompson-Minton

BRIGHTON & HOVE ALBION

MIDFIELDER

Nationality: English
Place of Birth: London
Date of Birth: 28 December 1973
Height: 5'6"
Club History: Tottenham Hotspur

Lee Thorpe

LINCOLN CITY

Forward

Nationality: English
Place of Birth: Wolverhampton
Date of Birth: 14 December 1975
Height: 6'0"
Club History: Blackpool
Horwich RMI

Michael Tomlinson

BARNET

Forward

Nationality: English
Place of Birth: London
Date of Birth: 15 September 1972
Height: 5'9"
Club History: Leyton Orient
St Albans

Gustaaf Uhlenbeek

IPSWICH TOWN

Forward

Nationality: Dutch
Place of Birth: Surinam
Date of Birth: 20 August 1970
Height: 5'9"
Club History: SV Tops

Patrick Vieira

WARD

Patrick Vieira takes on Sheffield United

Darius Vassell

ASTON VILLA

Forward

Nationality:	British
Place of Birth:	Birmingham
Date of Birth:	13 June 1980
Height:	5'10"

Patrick Vieira

ARSENAL

Midfielder

Nationality:	French
Place of Birth:	Dakar, Senegal
Date of Birth:	23 June 1976
Height:	6'4"
Club History:	Cannes AC Milan
Honours/Caps:	Premiership 1998 with Arsenal FA Cup 1998 with Arsenal Eight Caps for France

Irish maestro Liam Brady is probably the most revered midfielder the Gunners have had amongst their ranks. The Eire international could caress a ball like no other.

Arsenal's new kid on the block, Frenchman Patrick Vieira, may not have the same silky smooth skills as Brady, but there is no doubt that the north London faithful have taken him to their hearts.

Vieira is, according to the cliché, wholehearted. He tackles like a dervish and has a blistering shot with either foot. When Arsene Wenger purchased Vieira from Italian giants AC Milan, not much was known of him - that has all changed.

Vieira has proved a vital cog in a midfield that lacked a bit of flair. The man born in Dakar may not spray the ball around like the aforementioned Brady, but his energy and ball-winning skills make things happen.

Coming from a club such as AC Milan the weight of expectancy when Vieira arrived at Highbury was immense. He has dealt with it admirably, with the added bonus that he was given his international debut by France in a friendly against the Netherlands in February 1997.

Former French captain Luis Fernandez, once dubbed Vieira 'ET' - Extraordinary Teenager. At just 17, Vieira was playing for Cannes and a year later he became the French club's youngest ever captain.

After just six months in Italy, he became Arsene Wenger's first signing in August 1996 for £3.5m. The fans have taken to him admirably and for that, this hard-tackling player is appreciative.

Recalling his Premiership debut against Sheffield Wednesday, Vieira confessed: "I was very nervous coming on at half time. It was very difficult for me because we were losing one-nil and the fans must have looked at my name and seen that I had come from AC Milan and it was pressure for me.

"But the fans were good. It is one of my best memories so far because even when I was warming up, before I came on the field, the fans were singing my name."

The memories got even better for the Frenchman as his powerhouse performances ensured that the Gunners won the Premiership on 3 May 1998 with two games in hand after thrashing Everton 4-0 at Highbury. As if that was not enough, Vieira and Co. won the FA Cup Final against Newcastle United in the middle of May to capture the Double. The icing on the cake was a World Cup Winners' medal with France in July 1998.

Des Walker

SHEFFIELD WEDNESDAY

Defender

Nationality:	English
Place of Birth:	London
Date of Birth:	26 November 1965
Height:	5'11"
Club History:	Nottingham Forest Sampdoria
Honours/Caps:	League Cup 1989 and 1990 with Nottingham Forest 59 Caps for England

"You'll never beat Des Walker", was the chant from the terraces. And no one could. His searing pace was legendary as he left opposition markers in his wake.

Des Walker

Even now, at thirty-something, he is still churning out classy performances for Sheffield Wednesday.

It was at Nottingham Forest under the guidance of the unique Brian Clough that Walker burst onto the scene. He played 264 times for the East Midlanders, scoring his one and only league goal to date.

It was life with Brian which saw Italian club, Sampdoria, acquire the skills of Walker for £1.5m in August 1992. But he was to play just 30 times for the Italians. Just like Ian Rush, who had a nightmare at Juventus and Luther Blissett at AC Milan, the Italian game did not suit the talents of Hackney-born Walker.

For those who followed his career, his failure to make an impression in Italy came as a surprise because he had always looked at home against top-class opposition during his international career for England.

Some cynics indicated that his first-touch had never quite been good enough for him to survive in Italy's famed Serie A, a league noted for its top-notch skill factor. The steel city of Sheffield was to be the next stop for Walker.

Little is known of the very private Des Walker as he often shuns media attention. However, his exploits on the pitch are there for all to see.

Raymond Wallace

STOKE CITY

Defender

Nationality:	English
Place of Birth:	London
Date of Birth:	2 October 1969
Height:	5'6"
Club History:	Southampton Leeds United Swansea City Reading Hull City

Mark Walters

SWINDON TOWN

Forward

Nationality:	English
Place of Birth:	Birmingham
Date of Birth:	2 June 1964
Height:	5'9"
Club History:	Aston Villa Glasgow Rangers Liverpool Stoke City Southampton
Honours/Caps:	Scottish Premier Division 1989, 1990 and 1991 with Glasgow Rangers Scottish League Cup 1989 and 1991 with Glasgow Rangers FA Cup 1992 with Liverpool One cap for England

Not too many players plying their trade in the Nationwide League have the credentials of Mark Walters. He has literally seen and done it all. At Aston Villa, Glasgow Rangers and Liverpool he has played for three of the biggest clubs in the game. His wing play for Villa saw him transferred to Graeme Souness' Rangers for a cool £5m in December 1987. With Rangers, he put his hands on his first pieces of silverware - the Premiership - in three successive seasons - 1989 to 1991 - and the Scottish Cup twice in 1989 and 1991. Add his solitary England cap and an FA Cup winners' medal-gained when Liverpool beat Sunderland 2-0 in 1992, and you can see that Walters has gone some way to fulfilling his enormous early potential.

Paulo Wanchope

Paulo Wanchope

DERBY COUNTY

Forward

Nationality: Costa Rican
Place of Birth: Costa Rica
Date of Birth: 31 July 1976
Height: 6'4"
Club History: CS Heridiano, Costa Rica
Honours/Caps: Caps for Costa Rica

Costa Rica's Paulo Wanchope is the man who has put some South American rhythm into one of the Premiership's most improved teams - Derby County.

Wanchope, signed by the club for £800,000 in March 1997, has transfixed fans - and players - up and down the country with his pace and ball trickery. Some of his play has been nothing short of sensational. He is an entertainer who never ceases to leave you with a lasting memory.

Like most gifted, one-off players of his type there is another side of his play which can ultimately lead to head-scratching and frustration.

Derby manager Jim Smith, however, recognises that essentially he has a golden nugget on his hands. Smith says of Wanchope, "He's got that typical South American mobility, with very rubbery legs. His movement is very different to the normal British player's type of body movement."

Apart from his ability at ground level, Wanchope's ability in the air is equally startling. Manager Smith recalls one of his player's famous leaps: "He jumped as high as I have ever seen anyone jump to head a ball, probably about ten feet."

Paulo's prodigious leap must, in part, be due to the basketball scholarship he took at 17 when he was in San Diego. Two of his brothers are professional basketball players back home in Costa Rica.

Wanchope has gone on to emulate some of the sporting success of his brothers by representing Costa Rica in the qualifying tournament of France 98. Ironically, Wanchope was to come up against Derby team mate Deon Burton, who took the field for Jamaica. Both men tasted victory as the two nations battled it out for the right to play in France, but it must have led to some good natured banter in the very cosmopolitan Derby County dressing room.

At the end of February 1998, Derby recognised exactly what contribution Wanchope has made to the club's new found status. They offered him a new four-year contract, with manager Jim Smith declaring: "We are looking to secure the long term futures of a number of our players, but Paulo is top of our list. Paulo has an excellent record and has shown he has a few tricks up his sleeve as well."

Mark Warren

LEYTON ORIENT

Forward

Nationality: English
Place of Birth: London
Date of Birth: 12 November 1974
Height: 5'9"

Andy Watson

WALSALL

Midfielder

Nationality: English
Place of Birth: Leeds
Date of Birth: 1 April 1967
Height: 5'9"
Club History: Halifax Town
Swansea City
Carlisle United
Blackpool

Christopher Westwood

WOLVERHAMPTON WANDERERS

Defender

Nationality: English
Place of Birth: Dudley
Date of Birth: 13 February 1977
Height: 6'0"

Clyde Wijnhard

Spencer Whelan

CHESTER CITY

Defender

Nationality: English
Place of Birth: Liverpool
Date of Birth: 17 September 1971
Height: 6'1"
Club History: Liverpool

Devon White

NOTTS COUNTY

Forward

Nationality: English
Place of Birth: Nottingham
Date of Birth: 2 March 1964
Height: 6'3"
Club History: Arnold Kingswell
Lincoln City
Boston United
Bristol Rovers
Cambridge United
Queens Park Rangers
Watford

James Whitley

MANCHESTER CITY

Midfielder

Nationality: Welsh
Place of Birth: Zambia
Date of Birth: 14 April 1975
Height: 5'9"
Honours/Caps: Caps for Wales

Jeffrey Whitley

MANCHESTER CITY

Defender

Nationality: Northern Ireland
Place of Birth: Zambia
Date of Birth: 14 April 1975
Height: 5'8"
Honours/Caps: Caps for Northern Ireland

Justin Whittle

STOKE CITY

Defender

Nationality: English
Place of Birth: Derby
Date of Birth: 18 March 1971
Height: 6'1"
Club History: Celtic

Clyde Wijnhard

LEEDS UNITED

Forward

Nationality: Dutch
Place of Birth: Paramaribo, Surinam
Date of Birth: 1 November 1973
Height: 5'9"
Club History: Ajax
Groningen
RKC Waalnik
Willem II of Tilburg

Born in the same town in Surinam as his Leeds United team-mate, Jimmy Floyd Hasselbaink, Clyde Wijnhard is still trying to establish himself with the Yorkshire club.

Unlike Hasselbaink, Wijnhard is a quiet character who by his own admission is still trying to get to grips with such items as the Yorkshire accent and cuisine.

Until he feels completely at home, we are not likely to see the goal-scoring form which compelled previous Leeds boss, George Graham, to capture his signature.

A £1.5m signing for Leeds in the summer of 1998, Wijnhard scored 14 league goals to help Willem II of Tilburg into the UEFA Cup. Before that he had spells with Ajax, Groningen and RKC Waalnik.

John Williams

EXETER CITY

Forward

Nationality:	English
Place of Birth:	Birmingham
Date of Birth:	11 May 1968
Height:	6'2"
Club History:	Cradley Town Swansea City Coventry City Notts County Stoke City Wycombe Wanderers Hereford United Walsall

Martin Williams

READING

Forward

Nationality:	English
Place of Birth:	Luton
Date of Birth:	12 July 1973
Height:	5'9"
Club History:	Leicester City Luton Town

Michael Williams

BURNLEY

Midfielder

Nationality:	English
Place of Birth:	Bradford
Date of Birth:	21 November 1969
Height:	5'1"
Club History:	Maltby MW Sheffield Wednesday Huddersfield Town

Paul Williams

COVENTRY CITY

Defender

Nationality:	English
Place of Birth:	Burton on Trent
Date of Birth:	26 March 1971
Height:	5'11"
Club History:	Derby County Lincoln City
Honours/Caps:	Six Caps for England Under 21s

Not too many defenders have the goal-scoring record of Paul Williams. At his first club Derby County, Williams made 160 appearances and hit the back of the net 25 times.

That Williams played so many games for Derby is a tribute to his never-say-die qualities. Just four months into his Derby career he was farmed out to Lincoln City for a six-match loan period.

Coventry were to pay Derby £1m just prior to the 1995/96 season for his services. Like most Coventry players in recent times, Williams has been involved in countless last day battles to hold on to their Premiership status.

In between the challenge of helping his club stay up, Williams has earned himself half-a-dozen England Under-21 caps. He has also earned himself something of a tough guy reputation, with one or two disciplinary blips on his record. His year did not get off to the most wholesome of starts in January 1998 when he was sent off for allegedly tripping-up Arsenal's Dennis Bergkamp during a fiercely-fought battle at Highfield Road.

Unfortunately, Williams' style of play may have made him something of a marked man with officials.

Paul Williams

PLYMOUTH ARGYLE

Defender

Nationality: English
Place of Birth: Leicester
Date of Birth: 11 September 1969
Height: 5'6"
Club History: Leicester City
Stockport County
Coventry City
West Bromwich Albion

Paul Williams

SOUTHEND UNITED

Forward

Nationality: English
Place of Birth: London
Date of Birth: 16 August 1965
Height: 5'7"
Club History: Charlton Athletic
Brentford
Sheffield Wednesday
Crystal Palace
Sunderland
Birmingham City
Torquay United

Roger Willis

CHESTERFIELD

Forward

Nationality: English
Place of Birth: Sheffield
Date of Birth: 17 June 1967
Height: 6'2"
Club History: Grimsby Town
Barnet
Watford
Birmingham City
Southend United
Peterborough United

Clive Wilson

TOTTENHAM HOTSPUR

Defender

Nationality: English
Place of Birth: Manchester
Date of Birth: 13 November 1961
Height: 5'7"
Club History: Manchester City
Chester City
Chelsea
Queens Park Rangers

Doggedness and determination have always been the hallmark of the much travelled Clive Wilson's playing career. Consistency, too, has been a strong point for the Lancashire-born left-footed player.

Known as 'Mr Reliability', his various manager's have put his name first on their team-sheets.

In January 1998, it looked as if Spurs were prepared to give Wilson a free transfer. This alerted Kevin Keegan and Ray Wilkins at Fulham to the possibility of obtaining Wilson's experience and guile.

The sheer fact that Keegan and Wilkins, who were once lauded England internationals, wanted Clive's services, indicates that Wilson's abilities have not gone un-noticed by men who have played at the very highest level.

Wilson played 126 times for Manchester City, the club who also produced goalkeeper Alex Williams. That was a City side that, unlike today, gave rivals Manchester United a good run for their money in the trophy-winning stakes.

The 1997/98 season was a torrid affair for Wilson and Tottenham. Even though they possessed many internationals, Spurs could not get their act together, resulting in the constant threat of relegation. Wilson's form suffered along with the rest of the team. With the arrival of new boss George Graham, Wilson may now have a chance to shine once more.

Brian Wilsterman

OXFORD UNITED

Midfielder

Nationality: Dutch
Place of Birth: Surinam
Date of Birth: 19 November 1966
Height: 6'1"
Club History: Beerxchot, Holland

Anthony Witter

MILLWALL

Defender

Nationality: English
Place of Birth: London
Date of Birth: 12 August 1965
Height: 6'2"
Club History: Grays Athletic
Crystal Palace
Queens Park Rangers
Plymouth Argyle
Reading

Curtis Woodhouse

SHEFFIELD UNITED

Midfield

Nationality: English
Place of Birth: Beverley
Date of Birth: 17 April 1980
Height: 5'8"
Honours/Caps: England Under 21

Shaun Wray

SHREWSBURY TOWN

Forward

Nationality: English
Place of Birth: Dudley
Date of Birth: 14 March 1978
Height: 6'1"

Ian Wright

WEST HAM UNITED

Forward

Nationality: English
Place of Birth: London
Date of Birth: 3 November 1963
Height: 5'9"
Club History: Crystal Palace
Arsenal
Honours/Caps: League Cup 1993 with Arsenal
FA Cup 1993 and 1998 with Arsenal
Premiership 1998 with Arsenal
27 Caps for England

Former plasterer Ian Wright was destined to wear the red and white of Arsenal. After all, he was born in Woolwich and, from 1891 to 1914, the famous north London club was called Woolwich Arsenal.

Known to millions as the Gunners, the club purchased their biggest bullet of all from Crystal Palace for £2.5m in September 1991. Since then this most charismatic of players has gone on to be the scourge of every defence in the top flight and more importantly the club's record goal-scorer.

Almost everyone, football fan or not, has an anecdote to repeat about Wright, it seems. And I am no different. Yours truly was privileged enough to be at Highbury on September 13, 1997 when Arsenal beat newly promoted Bolton Wanderers 4-1. Wright was to score a hat-trick and thus claim the 50 year record once held by Cliff Basten of 178 League goals. The Arsenal faithful simply loved this unique figure who was hero-worshipped with the same gusto as former Highbury favourites Charlie George and Liam Brady.

Wright's disciplinary discretions have been well chronicled and there can be no doubt that on more than one occasion he has not helped his cause with a reckless challenge or statement. However, when it comes to goal-scoring he is up there with the likes of modern day heroes such as Ian Rush and Gary Lineker, both possibly the sharpest of shooters in recent times.

Since his move from Palace, he has gone from

Ian Wright breaks Cliff Basten's fifty-year record

Ian Wright

strength to strength. Some might not think it possible, but like his touch, Wright's confidence has improved under the spotlight of being at a major force in English football.

As he reaches the twilight of his career he is still in demand. At the start of 1998 World Cup year, the likes of Everton, Middlesbrough and Portuguese giants, Benfica, were all attempting to prise Wright away from Highbury. But he is not ready to hang up his boots just yet. One boot that is hanging up is the coveted Golden Boot, an accolade given to Europe's top scorer. Wright was the recipient of this honour in 1992 when he scored 24 league goals, just pipping the prolific Gary Lineker for the title.

As for that famed temperament, which has cost him his place in the team due to suspension and a few pounds in fines along the way, he confesses: "I've never been any different, I don't think I ever will be. I've tried to calm down, I've had counselling and all that but that's me, it's who I am. If I play without passion, it kills my game. The passion comes from inside. I've been in trouble for it, but if I look back at my career now, I wouldn't change a thing. The punishments, the criticism, none of it."

Wright's well known passion was there for all to see on the day that Arsenal won the 1997/98 Premiership. Nobody celebrated with more gusto than Wright after a Premiership-clinching 4-0 win against relegation-threatened Everton. Once the final whistle had gone, Wright bounded around the Highbury turf like a stag.

With the emergence of talented youngsters like Anelka and Wreh, Wright's first team opportunities were limited at the end of the Double winning season. With that in mind, Wright made a surprise transfer to West Ham United for a nominal fee in July 1998 and promptly continued his goal-scoring ways on his league debut for the Hammers on the opening day of the season. *RH*

Jermaine Wright

WOLVERHAMPTON WANDERERS

Forward

Nationality:	English
Place of Birth:	London
Date of Birth:	21 October 1975
Height:	5'9"

Dwight Yorke

MANCHESTER UNITED

Forward

Nationality:	Trinidadian
Place of Birth:	Tobago
Date of Birth:	3 November 1971
Height:	5'10"
Club History:	Signal Hill, Trinidad Aston Villa
Honours/Caps:	League Cup 1996 with Aston Villa 20 Caps for Trinidad and Tobago

Trinidad and Tobago's centre-forward should be labelled the Smiling Assassin. Dwight Yorke cannot be missed, his beaming wide smile epitomises the approach he takes to football and echoes the mantra recited by former Man United boss Sir Matt Busby - Yorke plays to enjoy himself.

It is not too often that Yorke is in trouble with officials as he plays the game with a tremendous attitude. The only time that one will see the ruthless streak in Yorke, is when he is in the opposition penalty box, devouring chances with relish.

At the end of the 1996/97 season Yorke had played exactly 200 times for Aston Villa hitting the net 61 times. In the last two completed seasons, Yorke had been the top-scorer (with 17 goals each time) for a club that has seriously underachieved to date.

Yorke's move to Manchester United had been the subject of the most furious on-off debate on soccer's always-busy grapevine for an interminable age. The completion of the deal meant that Yorke's quest to win top trophies on a regular basis was closer to fruition.

Dwight Yorke

Similar to United team-mate Andy Cole, this childhood friend of West Indies batsman Brian Lara, is not built in the traditional striker's mould. However, Yorke possesses pace, guile and enthusiasm to such good effect that the ball invariably ends up in the back of the net before defenders are able to establish what he is up to. Yorke, who has tasted League Cup success with Villa, established himself as a member of the team after his formative years at the club looked likely to end in disappointment. Villa are a big club and as such attract top quality players. Yorke was around when the likes of Dalian Atkinson and Dean Saunders were very much at the front of the club's pecking order.

Like John Barnes, Yorke owes much to former Villa boss Graham Taylor. Taylor, much maligned when he was in charge of England, was the man who discovered Yorke when Villa were on a trip to the Caribbean. Taylor saw the young man's ability and persuaded chairman Doug Ellis to part with just £10,000 to secure the services of Yorke from his local club, Signal Hill. With his haul of goals in the Premiership, European Champions League and Cup games for Manchester United in the 1998/99 season, some of Yorke's formerly sternest critics are claiming that United boss Alex Ferguson was the beneficiary of a similar bargain in securing the laughing Tobagon's services for a 'mere' £12.6 million. What a difference 25 goals can make to people's opinion of a player!

Dwight Yorke celebrates Manchester United's 2-0 win over Inter Milan